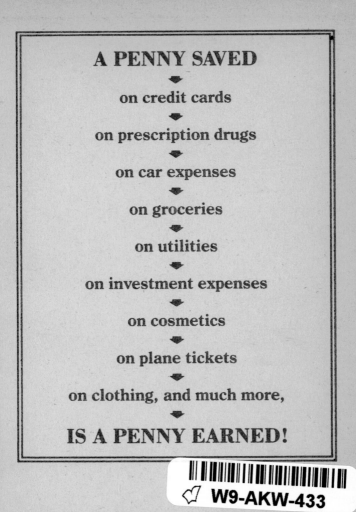

A PENNY SAVED

▼

on credit cards

▼

on prescription drugs

▼

on car expenses

▼

on groceries

▼

on utilities

▼

on investment expenses

▼

on cosmetics

▼

on plane tickets

▼

on clothing, and much more,

▼

IS A PENNY EARNED!

W9-AKW-433

For busy, successful people who want to live well, care about quality, and prefer not to cut back on the luxuries they enjoy right now, here is the book—now revised and updated for the 90s—that offers hundreds of ways you can do what you do, eat what you eat, wear the clothes you want to wear, and live the way you always have—but for less money than you're spending now.

PENNY PINCHING

Lee and Barbara Simmons

BANTAM BOOKS
NEW YORK · TORONTO · LONDON · SYDNEY · AUCKLAND

PENNY PINCHING
A Bantam Book

PUBLISHING HISTORY
Bantam edition published September 1991
Bantam revised edition / February 1993

ISBN 0-553-56013-1

Published simultaneously in the United States and Canada

Bantam Books are published by Bantam Books, a division of
Bantam Doubleday Dell Publishing Group, Inc. Its trademark,
consisting of the words "Bantam Books" and the portrayal of a
rooster, is Registered in U.S. Patent and Trademark Office and in
other countries. Marca Registrada. Bantam Books, 666 Fifth
Avenue, New York, New York 10103.

PRINTED IN THE UNITED STATES OF AMERICA

RAD   0 9 8 7 6 5 4 3 2 1

CONTENTS

v

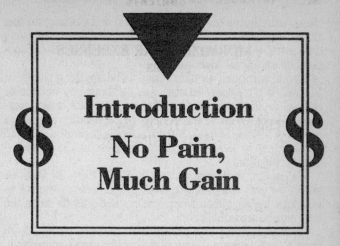

Introduction
No Pain, Much Gain

"Penny pinching is definitely back in style."

That was the first sentence of the first edition of this book, published in September 1991, and we see no reason to change it for this expanded, completely updated new version.

Actually, penny pinching is more than just "back in style." For millions of beleaguered middle-class Americans, it has become a necessity. No matter what happens to the national economy, it isn't likely that many of us will revert to the spend-it-like-there's-no-tomorrow habits we developed during the high-flying 1980s.

For the husband and wife who wrote this book, that's not bad news at all. Long before the recession of the early 1990s, when a change in jobs in 1988 sharply reduced our income, we began to learn, test, develop, and live with many of the penny-pinching strategies you'll find in the following pages. Our goal: to reduce our expenses without lowering our standard of living. We didn't want to buy cheap substitutes for the kind of food and clothing we had always enjoyed. We didn't want to spend hours of extra time each week doing things like bartering cents-off coupons or saving old aluminum foil.

To our surprise, we didn't have to do anything painful at all. You won't either. In our case, without any noticeable change in life-style, but taking into account major purchases in different years (a new car, a vacation abroad, a new roof for the house), our total living expenses were 15 percent less in 1991–1992 than they were in 1987–1988—despite inflation.

We expect to do just as well in 1993–1994. In fact, we know we will save hundreds of extra dollars, thanks to new tips we've gotten from readers and friends since the first edition was published.

"Penny pinching" is a phrase that has been passed down from a time when a penny was actually worth something. It's still a useful description of a worthwhile discipline, but we have concentrated on pinching dollars, not cents. Of course, if it is easy to take advantage of a 25 cents-off coupon on a $1.00 purchase, we do it. If we can easily save a few cents by switching to a product of equal quality, we do that, too. Cents still add up to dollars. But the operative words are "easy" and "quality"; we insist on both.

So this book is for busy, successful people who want to live well, care about quality, don't want to sacrifice a lot of precious leisure time, and prefer not to cut back on the luxuries they enjoy right now. What they need are ways to do what they do, eat what they eat, wear the clothes they want to wear, and live the way they always have—but for less money than it is costing them now.

How can you cut your weekly grocery bill by 10 to 15 percent without changing your family's eating habits? What are the no-pain ways to cut heating expenses? How do you buy the cheapest airline ticket possible? How can virtually anyone save up to 10 percent on automobile insurance even without changing insurance companies?

This book has some answers. You'll find money-saving tips on everything from cabbages and light bulbs to designer clothes and Treasury bills. How much can they save you? Perhaps hundreds, perhaps even thousands of dollars a year. For most people, changing just a few habits can lead to very substantial savings. What's more, although effective penny pinching requires a more organized approach than most people take to managing their money, many penny-pinching strategies will in the end actually save you time as well as money.

IT'S YOU AGAINST THEM

There's no question that the American consumer is protected by a number of local, state, and federal laws, better business bureaus, and regulations imposed by various industries. The question is, what do they really protect you from?

Usually there are safeguards in place against out-and-out fraud, theft, and outrageously obvious deception. But America is still very much a free enterprise society, still the country that invented most of the marketing techniques that have created consumer-driven economies around the world. So *caveat emptor*—let the buyer beware—is as useful a reminder in the 1990s as it was back in the days when our great-grandfathers were buying cure-all elixirs off the backs of horse-drawn carts.

To be a successful penny pincher, you must understand that you live in a society dominated by marketers who have devised countless sophisticated techniques to sell you what they want you to buy, when they want you to buy it, at the prices they want you to pay. They have created powerful brand images that persuade people to pay $1.50 for Soap A, which is identical except for packaging to 50-cent Soap B. They advertise "enormous savings" when things are priced at a normal markup and don't advertise at all when the same things are really on sale. They invent products you don't need but soon want. They even create holidays to sell their products; Mother's Day now generates hundreds of millions of dollars in sales each year. And they bombard you every day with thousands of messages that say buy, buy, buy.

There's nothing wrong with any of this. Mother's Day

has created thousands of new jobs. Selling, merchandising, advertising, and marketing are essential to a healthy national economy. But your own financial health depends on knowing when to turn off the sell messages and what tactics to employ when confronted with various purchase decisions.

Will anyone who reads this book want to or be able to use all of its strategies and tips? No. In fact, we've included a few ideas we can't or don't choose to use ourselves. Nevertheless, they have proved their usefulness with some of the dozens of other penny-pinching friends and acquaintances who have shared their own techniques with us.

Are you already likely to be aware of some of the ideas it recommends? Certainly. We debated including some of them because they seem to turn up in every magazine article about saving money. But if everyone knows that a cheap, homemade window washing mixture is just as effective as the expensive brand name products, how come tens of millions of dollars' worth of those products are still sold year after year?

Even people who already are successfully pinching pennies are bound to find a couple of new ways to save money—at least enough to pay for the book a few times over.

KEEPING SCORE

Whatever you save, it will be difficult to tell how much unless you know how you are spending your money right now. That means—uh-oh, here comes the b-word . . .

Yes, a *budget*. If the very thought of keeping records and setting priorities makes you shudder, skip the appendix to this book. You'll be avoiding the single most effective strategy in the battle to make your income go farther, but you don't absolutely need a budget to save money on what you eat, buy, invest, and do.

If, on the other hand, you already have a family budget, or are willing to start one, you have made a very wise decision. Financial planners trade stories about perfectly intelligent clients who, after years of never examining where their money went, begin keeping score and are shocked to discover how much they actually spend on certain things.

One Chicago stockbroker, for example, had fallen into the habit of buying seven different magazines on a regular basis from the newsstand in his office building. By subscribing to the same magazines and paying annual instead of single issue rates, he saved $435 a year. He cut his annual car expenses by nearly $2,500 a year by trading in his luxury convertible after three years instead of two. He adopted a simple new strategy for buying birthday and Christmas gifts and saved at least $1,000 a year.

You're nearly certain to be surprised by some of your own expenses in certain categories. And once you start a budget, you will probably set some different spending priorities. Even if you don't, experience has shown that people who keep budget records nearly always save money simply because they become far more aware of their spending habits.

The appendix will show you how to go about setting up a family budget. It is as quick, simple, and painless as possible. But it does require some effort and the cooperation of other family members. The hardest part of the process comes in the very beginning, when you have to pull together a lot of information and make decisions about priorities. Don't get discouraged. No matter what your family income, a good budget plan can put an end to those sleepless nights worrying about overdue bills. Most importantly, it can help you achieve your long-term financial goals.

This isn't a book you have to read in any particular order, but do spend some time in the main chapters before turning to the appendix. The whole idea of budgeting may be more appealing after you discover some specific ways to cut expenses in just about every budget category. Want to know how to spot the worst ripoffs in your supermarket? Where to buy name brand hosiery at a 50 percent discount? How to get more miles to the gallon no matter what kind of car you drive? Where to buy houseplants for a fraction of their usual cost? The best way to invest in mutual funds?

Whether they save you hundreds or thousands of dollars a year, we hope you'll find enough penny-pinching tips and strategies in these pages to help you live the good life for a lot less money.

THANKS TO FELLOW PENNY PINCHERS

who have amended and added to our tips and strategies since the first edition of *Penny Pinching* was published, especially Paul DeLuca, President of Telecom Consultants of Roslyn, New York, who shared with us his sound strategies for saving money on telephone service and equipment. Thanks also to Dan Green, whose publishing instincts are sharper than ever in the 1990s, and Becky Cabaza, an astute and considerate editor.

SHARE YOUR IDEAS WITH US

We will continue to expand and update *Penny Pinching* and invite you to send us any ideas you have. If we use them, you'll be acknowledged in future editions. Write to:

> Bantam Books
> Penny Pinching Editor
> 666 Fifth Avenue
> New York, NY 10103

PENNY PINCHING

Slashing Food and Grocery Bills

Have you ever given much thought to how a modern supermarket is organized? Probably not. But the corporations that own the supermarkets sure have, and so have Procter & Gamble, R.J. Reynolds, Coca-Cola, and the other giant package goods companies that make and market what's on the shelves.

After hundreds of millions of dollars and hours spent on continuing research and consumer testing, they have learned to stack the supermarket deck to accomplish one basic goal: to separate you from as much of your money as possible every time you set foot in a store.

Every element of a supermarket's design and floor plan is carefully planned to encourage as much unplanned "impulse" buying as possible. That's why the staple items needed by most shoppers are strategically spread all over the store; you are forced to walk through as many aisles as possible to get to them. Does that enormous display of one product at the end of an aisle signal a great bargain?

Sometimes, but more likely it is just a great promotion, usually paid for by the manufacturer.

The only way for you to win is to change the rules of the game so it is played your way, not theirs. The supermarket marketers want you to wander through their aisles making last minute decisions about tonight's dinner. Don't do it. Some of the strategies and tips in this chapter help you cut your grocery bills by avoiding impulse shopping. If you adopt most of them, annual savings of 15 percent or even more are a realistic goal. What's more, by cutting down the number of extra trips you make to the supermarket, you'll save time and a lot of aggravation as well.

The highest profits made by the giant food companies and supermarkets are in products that cost more because they promise to save you time and effort. To achieve maximum savings in your weekly food bill, cut out convenience foods altogether.

That's easier said than done, of course. It is cheaper to make your own soups than to buy cans, to bake a cake from scratch than to buy one from a bakery, to prepare a homemade chicken pot pie than to buy a frozen one. But few people these days have either the time or the inclination to do such things very often. It is worth paying for convenience—in some food categories, some of the time.

What is not worth paying for is the marketing ingenuity that has extended the convenience food concept to laughable extremes. Only a few of the more outrageous or pervasive examples are cited in the tips that follow. They will help you avoid some obvious ripoffs, but you can easily find hundreds more if you keep just a few rules of thumb in mind about shopping and paying for "convenience":

- The more removed from the original basic ingredients and the effort needed to prepare them, the more expensive the convenience product. For instance, making pancakes from flour, milk, eggs, baking powder, salt, sugar, and cooking oil is cheaper than buying a package of pancake mix, which is cheaper than frozen, premixed pancake batter, which is cheaper than frozen pancakes, which are cheaper than (the most recent gimmick), frozen, *microwavable* pancakes. Estimated cost of quality ingredients to make one dozen 4-inch pancakes from scratch: 34 cents. Cost of the same number of frozen microwave pancakes: $2.47.

- In any blind taste test, which kind of pancakes do you think would win? The addition of convenience characteristics nearly always means some loss of freshness, taste, texture, etc.
- Avoid convenience that is only a matter of smart packaging. Example: a can of chow mein vegetables sold in the same box with a pouch of soy sauce. Buy them separately. This kind of packaging provides no meaningful added convenience, just higher prices.
- Convenience is most expensive in small packages. Food marketers know that, as a group, busy single people are most likely to want no-hassle ways to prepare a meal. They charge especially high prices for "individual servings."

Prices used in this chapter were actual store prices at the time this book was going to press. Although the prices you will see on many items will no doubt be different, the price ratios between competitive choices probably won't change much at all.

▶ SHOP ONCE A WEEK

If you remember that impulse buying is the enemy, it makes sense to limit the number of times you face temptation. Besides, think of all the time (and gasoline and shoe leather) you waste by running to the supermarket for three or four items at a time.

You have to break this rule when you eat fresh fish or other highly perishable foods. But the principle is still sound: Try to buy everything you can on a once-a-week basis, and head right to the fish counter, the fresh bread case, or the fruit-and-vegetable section when you have to make a special trip.

▶ SHOP ALONE

Watch the next time you see a couple doing their weekly shopping together. The odds are good that she's filling her shopping basket with exactly the items on her checklist. He's roaming the aisles, reading the labels on all sorts of exotic stuff, and idly slipping jars of gourmet mustard and salsa into the basket. Kids are just as big a problem, and harder to argue with when they simply must have the new super-sugared technicolor cereal they just saw on TV.

▶ BEND AND STRETCH

Supermarkets tend to display the most popular, fastest-moving merchandise at eye level, encouraging impulse buying by making it easy. You may find better buys higher or lower on the shelves.

That bottom shelf may also hold items that cost less than they should. Clerks don't like bending over any more than you do and may not have repriced them.

▶ DON'T SHOP WHEN YOU'RE HUNGRY

You'll be far less likely to buy foods impulsively if you shop on a full stomach, not an empty one.

▶ USE UNIT PRICING

Some states, including California, Florida, Massachusetts, and New York, now require "unit price" information to be displayed on supermarket shelves, along with the price of the item. Especially given the often deceptive packaging practices of some food companies, unit price information is extremely helpful to consumers who want to know exactly how much they are getting for their money.

Example: Package A, priced at $1.50, sits right next to a competing brand of the same product, Package B, priced at $1.60. They are in exactly the same size package. Is A a better buy? No, because A actually contains 6 ounces and B 8 ounces. In a unit price state, the unit price per quart or pound as well as the price of the package must be displayed under each product: $4.00 a pound for A, $3.20 a pound for B.

It isn't difficult to do your own unit pricing if your state doesn't mandate it. Use a pocket calculator. When you are deciding between competitive packages, read the small print that tells you how much is inside. It will take a couple of seconds to divide the price by the amount to come up with a unit price.

▶ START WITH A LIST

There's no way to avoid making a few lists if you're serious about saving money. Grocery lists are probably the lists you'll use most often, and good ones can save you hundreds of dollars a year. The important impulse-avoiding rule is: *Never* shop without a grocery list in hand.

One way to have an efficient list each week is to first write down categories of food and groceries on a sheet or two of paper, in the same order that your supermarket's aisles are laid out. Leave space under each category to write down the items you may need each week, and photocopy this basic list. Keep a few dozen copies on hand.

Then, each week, before you go to the market, plan your menus and check your supplies, with preprinted basic list in hand. Write down the items you need in each category. Include brand names if you have strong preferences.

Many families keep a preprinted basic list on the refrigerator and make it each person's responsibility to note when, say, the eggs are running low or the last of the tuna fish cans has been used.

▶ BUY DRY STAPLES IN BULK

All you need is adequate storage space (someplace dry and cool) to save from 10 to 30 percent a year on items like toilet paper, paper towels, pasta, soap and detergents, toothpaste, and canned goods. Moving from your kitchen shelves and laundry to linen closets and bathrooms, make a list of items you are positive you use in case quantities.

Properly stored dried spaghetti, for example, lasts at least two years. If you use twenty-four one-pound packages a year, it makes sense to buy a case at a time.

Some supermarkets quietly give regular customers a

discount when they buy by the case. When you make up your first list, show it to the store manager and ask him what discounts he can offer. If necessary, you might politely suggest that you're prepared to go elsewhere for such discounts—and perhaps buy the rest of your groceries there, too. Since the list will probably represent quite a significant purchase, he'll want to keep you happy. Thereafter, when you may want to buy just a case at a time, remind him that he *always* gives you case discounts.

Whether or not you can get discounts on case purchases at your supermarket, if you have a warehouse club within driving distance, by all means check out prices there. It may be worth paying the annual membership fee most warehouse clubs charge and making a few special trips a year, if the discounts are better than your supermarket's. We saved 37 percent off the supermarket price of spaghetti recently by buying in bulk from our warehouse club.

Dividends: When you make special trips for bulk purchases, you'll be amazed at how much less you have to carry home from your weekly supermarket trip. And you will be far less likely to run out of the staple items you store in quantity.

▶ BUY SEASONALLY

Modern agriculture, transportation, and storage methods have made it possible to buy just about anything at any time of the year. But if you live in the Northeast, the $4.00-a-pint strawberries in December don't taste anywhere near as good as the 89-cent pint that's available in June. Anybody who eats corn on the cob except for the few weeks when locally grown corn is available is paying far too much for a vastly inferior vegetable. Penny-pinching corn-on-the-cob lovers gorge on it three or four times a week when it is at its best—and cheapest.

▶ BUY SEASONALLY FOR
YOUR FREEZER

When your favorite berries are in season and at their cheapest and best, why not buy a few extra boxes and freeze them? It's easy to do, and the frozen berries are both cheaper and superior to the sugar-loaded commercially frozen products you might otherwise buy. Simply clean and dry the berries—blue, straw, black, or raspberries—put them in a single layer on a cookie sheet and freeze them. When they are firm, pour them into a freezer bag and seal. They will be good for months.

Sample saving: November price of Birdseye frozen strawberries in sugar syrup, $1.69 for a 10-ounce package. Since the price of a quart of fresh strawberries when they are in season in our area is about the same amount, we pay at least 50 percent less for berries that we think are 500 percent better.

▶ SOME ADS WILL SAVE YOU MONEY

At least once a week, your local newspaper probably includes an advertising insert listing dozens of items on sale at your supermarket. It makes sense to use this ad when planning menus and making out your weekly grocery list. All supermarket chains make special quantity buys that allow them to price some items at genuinely lower prices than usual.

▶ GENERIC VERSUS BRAND NAME PRODUCTS

The standard advice about saving money on food and groceries involves substituting store brands and/or generics for national brands. The problem is, you prefer the taste or the quality of certain brands and don't want to give them up.

If you have a strong brand preference, one that you are sure of, stay with it and save other ways. If you are not convinced about such a preference, though, experiment. Try the least expensive option first. If you like it, why not save money by using it thereafter? If you don't, move up in price until you find an acceptable choice.

In many cases, you'll be equally satisfied with two or three similarly priced brands. When one of them is on sale or you have cents-off coupons saved for it, stock up.

In the last couple of years, many supermarket chains have moved away from the idea of selling generics but have improved the quality and variety of foods offered under their store brand names. If you haven't used them lately, you might want to try again. Many store-brand products are produced by major manufacturers whose own brands are made with the same ingredients in the same factories. The only differences are often just the labels and the prices.

▶ A FEW ALWAYS-BUY STORE BRANDS

We can't think of a single reason to buy brand name packages of certain staples. Typical savings:

- Store-brand granulated sugar: 5 pounds, $1.49 cents (37.3 cents per pound). Domino brand: 5 pounds, $2.29 (45.8 cents per pound).
- Store-brand all-purpose, enriched, bleached flour: 5 pounds, 99 cents (19.8 cents per pound). Pillsbury brand: 5 pounds, $1.29 (25.8 cents per pound).
- Store-brand iodized salt: 17.9 cents a pound. Diamond Crystal brand: 26.5 cents. But the price of Morton's brand at our warehouse club was 49 cents for a four-pound box (12.2 cents per pound).
- Store-brand distilled white vinegar: 49 cents a quart. Heinz brand: $1.09.
- Store-brand ammonia: 49 cents a quart. Parsons brand: $1.57.
- Store-brand regular bleach: 89 cents for two quarts. Clorox brand: $1.29.

▶ THE TRUTH ABOUT COUPONS

You get packets of them in the mail. You see them in national magazines. And Sunday newspapers are nearly always cluttered with inserts featuring dozens of money-saving manufacturer's coupons. Some people swear by them and brag about saving thousands of dollars a year in grocery bills. But unless you want to join a "trader's club" and spend hours a week searching for, clipping, organizing, and trading coupons, that kind of saving is unlikely. In fact, what many obsessive coupon-clippers are doing is "saving" money on a lot of products they otherwise wouldn't have bought.

Nevertheless, properly used, coupons can save you meaningful dollars nearly every week—not thousands a year, but quite possibly hundreds. You don't have to be obsessive about it, either. Here's what to do:

- Don't clip and use coupons for new products. You'll break this rule occasionally, but it is good advice ninety-nine times out of a hundred. All food manufacturers offer coupons to entice you to try their new products, but not many new products offer significant improvements over what's already available.
- Clip, save, and use coupons only for the brand names you normally buy or substitutes you know are acceptable. Do this on a regular weekly basis. It takes very little time to review the coupon advertising you receive when you look for and clip only the coupons for known, wanted brands. This way, you don't have to waste time reading the ads!
- Very often, when a brand name product is being "couponed," coupons appear in more than one place in a very brief period. Clip and save every coupon you see for a product you know you use. If it is for a perishable product, check the coupon expiration dates and use as many as feasible. If the product isn't perishable, use all the coupons you can and stock up.
- Infrequently, stores accept double coupons on certain products; that is, they allow two coupons to be used toward the purchase of a single item. If so, it may be worthwhile to buy another copy of the newspaper in which the coupon appears.
- Stores also sometimes honor a different kind of "double coupon" by allowing a 25-cent coupon, for instance, to be redeemed for 50 cents.
- Keep all the coupons you clip in one envelope or in an old checkbook cover. If this becomes unmanageable, divide the coupons by category into a few more envelopes.
- It takes just a couple of seconds per coupon to mark the expiration date of each with a yellow grease pencil or

felt-tip pen. Once you do, you'll spot that date whenever you look at the coupon. Missed a date? There are greater tragedies. Throw it away.

■ Review your coupons quickly before you make out your weekly shopping list. Then put an X next to each item you plan to buy for which you have a coupon. As you select each of these products, pull the coupons out of their storage envelopes and paper clip them together for easy retrieval at the checkout counter.

■ Check the before-coupon price before you buy a product. Every once in a while, you may find that that price minus the coupon value is still higher than the price of the uncouponed but acceptable substitute right next to it.

▶ CASH IN ON REFUND OFFERS

Coupons you redeem in stores save you money. Manufacturers' refund offers give you cash. For some reason, many people who use coupons in stores never take advantage of refund offers. Yet it is really quite an easy way to pick up a few extra dollars a month without much effort— perhaps as much as a few hundred a year, if you want to devote some extra time and energy to it. We never have, but if you are interested, your library probably has a book or two about how to achieve maximum savings by using both coupon and refund offers. (Look for *How to Shop Like a Coupon Queen* by Michelle Easter, Berkley Books. Michelle Easter is also the publisher of a monthly refunding newsletter. For information, send a self-addressed stamped envelope to Refunding Makes Cents, P.O. Box R, Farmington, Utah 84025.)

You'll find refund offers in the same places as coupons, as well as on forms attached to the product itself. Because it costs you a first class stamp to mail the refund form (along with proof of purchase—normally a specific panel from the product's label), it would be silly to return one to get a 35-cent check. Most manufacturers' refund offers are therefore for at least $1.00. Exchanging 29 cents for a dollar or two makes perfectly good sense to us, even taking into account the typical eight-week delay until the manufacturer's check is sent to you.

▶ JOIN A WAREHOUSE CLUB

The first warehouse club was opened by the Price Company in San Diego in 1976. Offering a hodgepodge of merchandise—including brand name food and groceries—at deeply discounted prices, it limited its customers to small business owners and government employees and charged them an annual membership fee.

The warehouse club phenomenon has spread to just about every part of the country, and the Price Company's Price Club now has a number of competitors, including Costco, Pace, Sam's Wholesale Club, SuperSaver, and others. There are more than 450 warehouse club outlets nationwide, some of them doing over $100 million annually. Typically, they charge a $25.00 membership fee and, although all have some restrictions on who can be a member, most people find a way to qualify for membership in one category or another.

Should you join a warehouse club? The best way to decide is to visit one first. Either call ahead to confirm that the club will allow you to look the place over before joining, or accompany a friend who is already a member. But before you make the trip, make a list of all of the staple grocery, food, and hardware items you use in bulk or large quantities. Then go to your normal sources for these items, and price them. (*Important:* Very often, warehouse clubs sell only larger packages that are unavailable in other retail stores, so make sure you note unit pricing of food and groceries—the cost per ounce, quart, or pound.)

Have you also been considering buying a new small appliance of any kind? New tires? Sheets? Towels? Garden hose? You are likely to find just about anything for sale in a warehouse club, including major national brand names, but you won't find the variety of choices within product categories that you will in other stores. Knowing beforehand the competitive prices of anything you might purchase is important, because incredible buys are likely to sit right next to items that can be purchased elsewhere for even less.

In our experience, however, it isn't likely that a careful

shopper will make a big mistake at a warehouse club. Nearly all of the food and grocery prices we have checked at our warehouse club are at least competitive, and we save from 20 percent to as much as 60 percent on some items.

Warehouse clubs are profit-making businesses, not consumer clubs. Don't get carried away, buying things in bulk that will ultimately spoil or will never get used. Also, be wary of two or three disparate items shrink-wrapped together and sold for one price (a cookbook with a Teflon fry pan, for instance). This kind of merchandising is how the clubs enhance "perceived value," but do you really want both items? If not, the combined price is certainly not a bargain.

▶ AVOID SUPERMARKETS FOR SOME NON-FOOD ITEMS

As supermarkets grow larger and stock a wider variety of products, you can get in the habit of using them to buy products that are cheaper elsewhere. In our area, discount drug stores nearly always have lower prices on toothpaste and aspirin, for instance. Light bulbs are cheaper at Home Depot. If we aren't able to buy in bulk at our warehouse club, we try to stock up on items sold in discount stores so we don't find ourselves "running out" and buying them one at a time from our supermarket.

▶ SHOP AT BAKERY THRIFT SHOPS

A number of national and regional bakeries have thrift outlets that sell their day-old products at 40 to 50 percent off retail prices. Don't buy stale bread. But certain cakes, cookies, muffins, and buns are as good a day later as they are when fresh-baked. Often, these outlets also sell at big discounts packages of cookies that may contain a couple of broken ones. In our area, Entenmann's and Pepperidge Farms outlets are particularly good; Arnold's, Oroweat, and Wonder Bread operate outlets in other parts of the country.

▶ COMPARE LOOSE VERSUS "BY-THE-BAG" PRODUCE PRICES

Kept in a cool, dry place, potatoes will keep for about a month. If you will use 10 pounds in that time, buying a 10-pound bag (as we recently did for $1.49) beats buying loose (69 cents a pound). The loose potatoes were larger, but we don't find it inconvenient (at a saving of 54 cents a pound) to use an extra couple from the bag when we are baking them.

Yellow onions, which will keep for up to a month, were 59 cents a pound loose, $1.19 for a 3-pound bag. Per pound difference: 19 cents.

▶ MAKE YOUR OWN BABY FOOD

Few parents would want to give up the convenience of prepared baby foods altogether, but you can save a significant amount of money, particularly when fresh fruits and vegetables are in abundant supply, by making baby meals from the same foods you'll be eating. Just put them in a mini food processor after cooking. Use fresh foods, and don't mix two or more together—babies prefer single flavors. (For some excellent recipes and advice on making and storing your own baby food, see *The Complete New Guide to Preparing Baby Foods* by Sue Castle, Bantam Books.)

▶ BUY DRY PASTA

The "fresh" pastas sold in supermarkets don't taste any better—and often taste worse—than their dry equivalents at one fourth the price. Don't confuse these so-called fresh pastas with freshly made pastas you have enjoyed at good restaurants or in a gourmet Italian cook's home; the stuff on supermarket shelves contains preservatives.

▶ SAVE WITH FRESH VERSUS CANNED OR FROZEN VEGETABLES

There's a reason to buy one can of mushrooms that will keep indefinitely and can be used at the last minute in an emergency. Otherwise, why not buy fresh? Price per pound: $2.79. Price for a 7-ounce jar (4 ounces drained) of Green Giant whole mushrooms, $1.49 ($5.96 a pound).

Not every example is as dramatic, and store-brand frozen green beans may not cost significantly more than fresh green beans at certain times of the year. But there's normally some kind of saving, and the extra time devoted to washing and cutting fresh beans always seems to us to pay off when they are served.

▶ CONVENIENCE RIPOFFS: PRODUCE SECTION

- A 16-ounce cellophane package of chopped cabbage labeled "Fresh Cole Slaw." Price: $1.59. Three feet away: cabbages at 49 cents a pound. Estimated time to chop a pound of cabbage: 90 seconds. Hourly rate being charged: $44.00 for the convenience of prechopped greens that are usually dried out.
- An 8-ounce package of "crinkle-cut" carrot "chips" (¼-inch slices of raw carrot). Price: $1.29. Two feet away: a bunch of carrots (1½ pounds). Price: 99 cents. Weight after removal of tops and peeling off outer skin: 18 ounces. Adjusted price for 8 ounces: 44 cents. Estimated time to remove tops, peel, and slice 8 ounces of carrots: three minutes. Hourly rate: $17.00 for the convenience of carrots that always look inedible to us.
- A 16-ounce package of celery hearts. Price: $1.89. In the adjacent bin, bunches of celery (weight from 24 to 32 ounces) for 99 cents. Since all that distinguishes the two kinds of celery is a simple swipe of a chopping knife (removing the leafy top part of the celery; estimated time: 5 seconds), the price of convenience was at least $648 an hour.

▶ CONVENIENCE RIPOFFS: DAIRY SECTION

- A pound of grated Parmesan Grana cheese was $9.99 whole, $10.99 grated. At high prices like these, though,

you want the cheese at its best, and it will stay fresher and last longer in block form. Grating just the amount you need each time you use it takes seconds extra.
- A worse ripoff: A 1-pound block of Wisconsin sharp cheddar was $2.99, the same cheese shredded was $2.59 per 8-ounce package—$2.19 more per pound.
- And another: presliced Swiss cheese, $5.29 per pound. A 1-pound block of the same cheese: $3.49. If you want thin, evenly sliced cheese or cold cuts and your supermarket has a delicatessen department, you might pay a lower premium for convenience by shopping there rather than buying presliced packaged brand name products.
- Minute Maid orange juice made from concentrate: $2.99 for two quarts in the dairy section. Six aisles away in the frozen food section: Minute Maid orange juice concentrate: $1.99 for a can that makes two quarts. Actually, we find it more convenient to store a few small cans in the freezer and defrost one as needed than to carry the bulky 64-ounce containers home from the market. We also like the environmental aspects of cutting back on unnecessary nonrecyclable plastic containers.

▶ CONVENIENCE RIPOFFS: BABY FOOD

This is a section of the supermarket where the price of convenience and individual servings is particularly high. If you don't want to make a lot of your own baby food (and food processors, blenders, and food mills make it very simple with many foods), at least compare prices with what's offered in other sections. For instance, a 4-ounce jar of Gerber's strained apple juice was 39 cents ($3.12 a quart). Store-brand apple juice was 99 cents a quart and Mott's was $1.99; both were made from concentrate. Nature's Own brand, not made from concentrate, was $1.99 a quart. If you think it necessary, you can strain any of these by pouring the juice through a couple of layers of cheesecloth.

▶ CONVENIENCE RIPOFFS:
RICE, PASTA, CEREAL

A 10-pound bag of Uncle Ben's converted rice cost $5.69 at a warehouse club ($8.47 at a supermarket). A 7-ounce package of the same rice in four "boil-in" bags cost $1.19. Per pound premium for the convenience of boil-in bags: $2.15 (versus warehouse club), $1.87 (versus supermarket).

- Five pounds of macaroni cost $2.19 (44 cents a pound) at a warehouse club. The supermarket price of a 7¼-ounce package of Kraft's "Macaroni and Cheese" was 69 cents ($1.57 a pound). For the $1.13 per pound difference, you can buy a lot more and a lot better cheese than the salty stuff inside the pouch included in the convenience package.

- Quaker Oats oatmeal comes packaged in different "with fruit" flavors, ten pouches of 2.5 ounces each at a price of $2.69 or 26.9 cents a serving. Quick Quaker Oats are $3.19 for 42 ounces ($1.22 per pound). Add your own fruit and save 14.7 cents a serving.

- Any cereal with fruit in the box is invariably more expensive than the ingredients warrant, and the fruit is a pale imitation of the real thing. At least in our experience, the raisins in those cereal boxes are often hard and dry. We buy and add our own.

- While on the subject of cereals, you should also check prices out at health food stores. Very often, because they buy and sell bran and other cereals, grains, flours, beans, rice, pasta, and other staples generically and in bulk quantities, you'll find prices well below those in your supermarket.

▶ CONVENIENCE RIPOFFS:
FROZEN FOODS

The frozen foods section of any supermarket is a virtual cornucopia of convenient ripoffs. Just a few:

- A 4-ounce "single serve" package of Ore-Ida microwave crinkle-cut french-fried potatoes. Price: 69 cents ($2.76 a pound). Price per pound of a 10-pound bag of russet potatoes: 12 cents. Price of one pound of potatoes (if you cook one for you, you can't often buy in large quantities), 33 cents. As the saying goes, any way you slice it . . .

- Gorton's Microwave Baked Scrod with Bread Crumbs: $3.19 for a 6-ounce package, or $8.51 a pound. But since the bread crumbs, by our measure, amounted to about 2 ounces of the weight, the price for the frozen scrod was actually $12.76 per pound. Fresh scrod was priced at $4.99 a pound.
- Like buttered vegetables? Add the butter yourself. A 10-ounce package of frozen small peas in a pouch with butter was $1.79, $1.00 more than the same size package of butterless peas.

▶ SAVE ON MEAT AND POULTRY

There aren't many bargains in the meat and poultry cases of supermarkets. Many people save by joining a service that makes home deliveries of frozen meats, buying in quantity for storage in home freezers. We tried such a service years ago, didn't like the quality of the frozen food we got, and found we always had the wrong quantities of the wrong things. Also, like many people, we have cut back on the amount of meat we eat these days, so buying in large quantities doesn't make sense for us.

If you have a large family, though, you might want to check into such a service. Look in your Yellow Pages or get recommendations from friends. You should be able to save between 10 and 20 percent by buying this way.

We look for sales and often buy and freeze for future use extra packages of boneless chicken breasts. We realize we pay for the convenience of having the breasts boned, but when they are on sale this is a minimal expense. We try not to pay for the convenience of really easy butchering, however. Our supermarket, for instance, was recently selling "pork kabobs"—chunks of pork loin— for $5.49 per pound and the pork loin itself for $4.49.

There are many other examples of this kind of convenience packaging in the meat case, and you'll have to decide if the convenience is worth the price in each individual case. We have found, for instance, an easy way to save about $2.00 per pound on something we cook quite often. The recent price per pound of a fresh whole turkey breast was $2.49. Same day price of fresh "turkey cutlets" (a fancy name for sliced turkey breast): $4.99 a pound.

To make your own cutlets (time expended to debone, slice, and flatten a 5-pound breast: 4½ minutes), remove skin from breast. Using a sharp knife, cut along the top of the breastbone, keeping the knife blade as close to the breastbone as possible, until one entire half breast is separated from the bone. Repeat on the other side. Then place the cut side down on a flat surface and, cutting across the grain, cut each breast into half-inch slices. Put the slices between sheets of waxed paper and pound flat.

▶ SKIP "NAME BRAND" CHICKEN

From time to time, we test out a "name brand," but we have yet to detect any consistent difference in flavor or quality among different labels of chicken and chicken parts. If it looks fresh and wholesome, buy the cheapest brand available and let someone else pay for the cute advertising.

▶ MARINATE LESS COSTLY CUTS OF MEAT

Substituting less expensive round steak for sirloin (just one example) doesn't have to mean giving up tenderness or flavor. Experiment with recipes that call for marinating the meat, and extend the length of marinating time called for in the recipe.

You can often cut down on the amount of liquid called for in a marinade, and therefore its cost, if you marinate in a self-closing plastic bag instead of an open, flat pan. Less mess, too.

▶ MAKE YOUR OWN SALAD DRESSINGS

Homemade salad dressings, without chemicals and preservatives, taste better than brand name prepared salad dressings. That's just an opinion, of course, but if you share it you can save from 25 to 90 percent on salad dressings without spending more than five extra minutes a week mixing your own. Try the recipes in any good general cookbook. Here are three that we use constantly:

- *Spicy sweet and sour dressing.* Mix 1 cup salad oil, ⅓ cup red wine vinegar, ¼ cup chili sauce, ¼ cup mayonnaise, 1 tablespoon sugar, 2 crushed garlic cloves, pinches of salt and cayenne pepper to taste. Shake all ingredients in a jar, chill well and always shake before using. Will keep for a couple of weeks.
- *Sort-of-French dressing.* Mix ½ cup salad oil, ⅓ cup red wine vinegar, 1 teaspoon dry mustard, 1 teaspoon sugar, 1 teaspoon dry basil or 2 teaspoons finely minced fresh basil, ½ teaspoon garlic powder, ½ teaspoon freshly grated black pepper, ½ teaspoon salt. Chill and shake well before using. Will keep for a couple of weeks.
- *Sort-of-Italian dressing.* Because it will keep for months, we make this in larger quantities. Mix 1½ cups salad oil, 1 cup white vinegar, ¼ cup sugar, ½ cup finely minced onion, 3 teaspoons dry basil, 3 teaspoons oregano. Chill and shake well before using.

Storage: Use old glass jars and bottles that have clean lids that still close tightly. Sterilize them first by simmering (just below boiling temperature) jars and lids separately in a large pot for fifteen minutes.

▶ USE A FOOD PROCESSOR

Why buy bread crumbs when you can make them in seconds from frozen crusts of stale bread you would otherwise have thrown out? A lot of the prepared and processed foods you may be buying now at your supermarket can be made for a lot less money with a food processor. Many processors come with free recipe books that explain how to buy when foods are at their lowest prices, then process and freeze them for later use. Processors are also useful for converting leftovers into appetizing soups, sauces, and casseroles. A good blender will do practically the same job.

▶ START YOUR OWN CONTAINER GARDEN

Too many people think that vegetable gardening is an all-or-nothing proposition, that you can't have a garden unless you cultivate a large area and spend hours a week seeding, weeding, and spraying. Not so. Container gardening allows you to plant enough tomato plants in a half barrel to keep a family of four well supplied with delicious tomatoes for a few weeks—at one tenth the cost of store-bought. A container or windowsill herb garden is easy to tend and is a real money saver. And if you do have the land available and can devote a couple of hours a week to a small vegetable garden, even 100 square feet is enough to save hundreds of dollars a year.

▶ DON'T TAKE OUT, COOK AHEAD

Anyone with a full-time job knows how tempting it is to stop by a take-out place on the way home from work, or to have dinner delivered. But these are expensive options. Instead, when you are in the mood to cook, prepare such things as casseroles and soups in quantity. Freeze them in portions just big enough for one meal, then bake or microwave a quick, no-fuss dinner whenever you don't feel like cooking.

▶ CHANGE OFFICE EATING HABITS

How much do you spend a year on morning coffee and donuts? How much on take-out sandwiches you eat at your desk? If you work in an office in a big city, the answer could easily be as much as $30.00 a week—$1,500 a year. You can save at least 75 percent by making your own coffee (share a $14.95 coffeemaker and cleanup chores with two or three other penny pinchers in your office) and bringing lunch from home.

▶ TRY A POSTHARVEST "BAKE DAY"

Invite friends to buy a bushel of apples with you in the fall when they are at their cheapest. Buy flour and other ingredients at bulk discounts, then bake enough pies to stock your freezers to last through the winter. If you have a large freezer, the strategy works just as well with lots of other ingredients that are cheap when they are in season.

▶ INVEST IN A GOOD BASIC COOKBOOK

Many people who have grown up with prepared convenience foods think that cooking is terribly complicated and time-consuming. If you are one of them, a big basic cookbook, one that explains everything, including how to boil water, is likely to persuade you otherwise.

Perhaps you'll go back to the convenience products, but with the step-by-step guidance in these books you can at least experiment. Try making a few cakes, pies, pastries, cookies, biscuits, or muffins from scratch instead of from boxes. Make your own spaghetti and pizza sauces instead of buying them in cans and jars. Prepare fresh instead of frozen vegetables.

Especially with the labor-saving appliances now available, preparing and cooking foods is far less time-consuming now than it was a generation ago. And as convenience food marketers add gimmicks to their products, prices continue to escalate. A "back to the basics" approach will pay off in better tasting, more nutritious, additive-free meals, in less environment-threatening packaging waste, and in lower food costs.

The book we turn to first for advice is *The New Doubleday Cookbook* by Jean Anderson and Elaine Hanna (Doubleday & Company, $29.95 list price). It is the most expensive of the good basic books (*The Joy of Cooking* and *The Good Housekeeping Cookbook* are other good choices), but it is also mammoth—967 pages long and truly comprehensive.

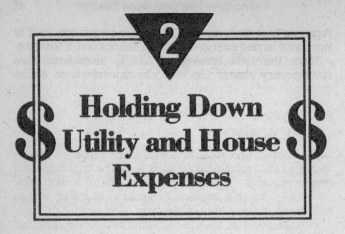

Holding Down Utility and House Expenses

Despite the progress we have made in the past two decades, Americans remain the greatest wasters of energy in the world. Although we have seen our energy costs soar since 1972, and have become far more aware of environmental costs as well, habits developed over generations of cheap and seemingly limitless energy have died hard.

If you own an average size home and haven't yet focused on saving energy, you should find it easy to lop a few hundred dollars a year off your energy bill. The first thing you should know is what your energy dollar buys. Based on national averages, the Department of Energy estimates that 48 percent of it goes to heat and/or cool your house. An additional 16 percent is spent on heating water. Refrigerators and freezers use 12 percent. The remaining 24 percent goes into lighting, cooking, and running appliances.

This chapter is filled with tips that will help you cut your costs in each one of these areas. It will also tell you where to go for more technical advice on major projects such as replacing heating equipment or installing solar energy. For tips about buying energy-saving appliances, see Chapter 4.

Since the 1984 breakup of AT&T, there have been revolutionary changes in how you buy telephone equipment and services. Like it or not, you must now choose from a bewildering array of equipment, services, competing long-distance carriers, and billing options. For most families, the difference between the right and wrong choices about telephone service easily adds up to a minimum of $10.00 a month. Heavy users should be able to save hundreds of dollars a year by adopting some of this chapter's strategies.

Other tips in this chapter can be categorized as general "household hints." There are a number of good books, including those by Mary Ellen and Heloise, that list an astonishing array of hints on everything from treating diaper rash to making bookends out of two upholstered bricks.

This book doesn't attempt to duplicate what's in the household hints books. Our tips are limited to those we genuinely believe may save you dollars, not pennies, and don't involve a lot of extra time. Not that spending the time to do it yourself isn't the best as well as the most obvious way to save money when you own a house. If you always pay a plumber to fix a leaky faucet or a painter to put a new coat on your bedroom walls, you are either very rich or very foolish. You most certainly are not a penny pincher.

Learning how to do a few basic repairs around the house is not that difficult, even if you've never held a hammer. Buy a good, well-illustrated, single-volume do-it-yourself reference and turn to it first when something needs fixing. (We depend on *Reader's Digest Complete Do-It-Yourself Manual*.)

The first edition of this book recommended another resource that you should cultivate and use—your local hardware store. We have carried leaky faucets into ours and gotten advice that saved us a $60.00 plumbing bill for the price of a 35-cent washer. We're grateful and still buy there. But in the past year we have discovered that the giant Home Depot discount warehouse in our area also has some knowledgeable salespeople available to answer similar questions, along with consistently low prices and an enormous range of items in stock.

The few do-it-yourself-type tips in this chapter won't help you fix anything that needs major repair work. They may help, however, when something is so simple to fix that you would be seriously embarrassed had you called in a service person. Finally, you'll find tips that suggest cheap substitutes for expensive brand name products everyone uses around the house.

▶ SAVE 20 PERCENT ON WATER HEATING

Hot water is usually the second most expensive item on your total annual energy bill, right after heating the house. Consider doing these simple things and save at least 20 percent a year:

- Buy and install a programmable water heater control (about $75.00). How often do you need hot water at 3:00 A.M.?
- Buy and install an insulation blanket (about $15.00) to put on your water heater, especially if it feels very warm to the touch. All water heaters lose some heat through the walls of the tank. Depending on how well yours is insulated, a blanket could save up to 10 percent on your water heating bills.
- Lower your water heater temperature from 140 degrees F to 125 degrees F. This is more than hot enough for bathing and washing clothes. *Note:* Check first to see if the lower temperature meets the specifications for your dishwasher. Some require the higher temperature.
- Wait until your dishwasher is full before turning it on. One less load per week can save you as much as $50.00 a year.
- Fix any faucet drip, of course, but fix a hot water faucet drip immediately. It could easily add $25.00 a month to your fuel costs.

- Replace your showerhead with a low-flow head (about $20.00). This is simply a matter of unscrewing the old showerhead and installing a new one. Two people each showering five minutes a day will use over 18,000 gallons of hot water a year. With a low-flow head, you can cut that by as much as 8,000 gallons and pay for the new showerhead in less than three months.
- Try using a cold water detergent and cold water for most laundry loads. We've found that only very dirty or greasy laundry needs hot water.
- Install aerators in bathroom and kitchen faucets. They cost a few dollars apiece and, by reducing the amount of hot water used, pay for themselves within a year.
- Insulate hot water pipes. This will reduce the heat lost through the pipe walls as hot water flows from your water heater to the faucet. You will also save gallons of water by reducing the time needed to bring hot water to the faucet when you first turn the water on.

▶ LIGHT A CANDLE NEAR YOUR DOORS AND WINDOWS

The easiest way to check on whether your doors and windows need better weatherstripping and/or caulking is to move a lighted candle around the frames. You'll know immediately if air is passing through.

▶ CAULK AND WEATHERSTRIP

Caulking and weatherstripping two doors and a dozen windows should cost less than $40.00. Savings in annual energy costs could amount to 10 percent or more.

▶ INSULATE FLOORS OVER UNHEATED SPACES

Even in newer homes, insulation during construction was sometimes skipped over unheated spaces such as garages and crawl spaces. Any do-it-yourself reference will show you how easy insulating is to do, and you'll cut energy bills significantly. One of the best short do-it-yourself guides is free from Owens-Corning Fiberglass when you call 800-438-7465 and ask for their *Homeowner's Guide to Insulation and Energy Savings*.

▶ CONSIDER A HEAT PUMP

If you use electric furnace heating, look into a heat pump system using thermal energy from outside air for both heating and cooling. A whole house unit will cost more than $2,000, but may cut your heating and cooling costs by 30 to 40 percent.

▶ BUY HEATING OIL IN THE SUMMER

You can nearly always save 10 to 20 percent by having your tank filled during the summer months, instead of waiting for a regular delivery in the fall.

▶ TAKE ADVANTAGE OF UTILITY OFF-PEAK USAGE DISCOUNTS

In some areas of the country, electric utilities offer residential customers cheaper rates at certain times of the day. If yours is one of them, it is easy to run your dishwasher, washer, and dryer at off-peak times and cut your electric bills by a few dollars a month.

▶ USE CEILING FANS ALL YEAR ROUND

Ceiling fans use less than one tenth as much electricity as a room air conditioner. What many people don't know is that in rooms where ceilings are at least eight feet high, they are extremely versatile energy savers in both winter and summer.

In the summer, if it is too hot for a ceiling fan alone to keep a room comfortable, you will still save money by turning the fan on along with the air-conditioning. Because a good ceiling fan can make you feel from five to seven degrees cooler, you can set the thermostat of your air conditioner that much higher.

In the winter, turn the fan on after first reversing the direction of the blades (make sure you install fans with reversible motors). Because warm air tends to rise toward the ceiling, the fan will keep heat where you want it—lower in the room. You'll be able to set thermostats lower and still feel comfortable. The higher the ceiling, the more significant the savings.

▶ USE VENTILATING FANS SPARINGLY

One of those ventilating fans in the kitchen or bathroom is capable of blowing away a houseful of warmed or cooled air in just one hour. Turn them off quickly after they've done their jobs.

▶ OPEN A WINDOW NEAR YOUR FIREPLACE

It may seem strange, but if you open a window near the fireplace by about half an inch, air needed by the fire will be drawn from the outside instead of from the (expensive) heated air in the house.

▶ CLOSE YOUR FIREPLACE DAMPER

Once the fire is completely out, close the damper immediately. It can let up to 8 percent of the heat in your house exit via the chimney.

▶ WEAR A SWEATER INSIDE

Most people discover they are just as comfortable wearing a sweater with the thermostat set at from 66 to 68 degrees F as they are without one with the thermostat set from 68 to 70. You will save about 2 percent of your heating bill for each degree you lower the thermostat.

▶ GET CREATIVE WITH YOUR THERMOSTAT

Turn it to its lowest setting when you'll be away for even a couple of days. Turn it down before a party—a crowd will generate heat. If you don't have a clock thermostat that you can preset for lower temperatures at night, it is a good investment.

▶ USE SHADES AND DRAPERIES

During cold weather, open them on sunny windows during the day and close them at night. During warm weather, do the opposite.

▶ AIM AIR CONDITIONER VENTS UP

Hot air rises, cold air falls. Air circulation will be more efficient and energy costs less if you aim an air conditioner's vents up. Keep the unit away from drapes, furniture, doors, whatever might interfere with air circulation. Also make sure it isn't near appliances that heat up or in direct sunlight (the outside part of the unit as well as the inside).

▶ GET A FREE ENERGY AUDIT

There are a number of ways to save on energy costs involving such things as boiler efficiency, but it is best to get advice that can be applied to your own specific needs. In most areas, there is an easy way to do this. Call your local utility and ask if they will send a conservation expert to your house to do a complete energy review. Many utilities offer this service without charge; others charge a small fee. It is always a worthwhile expenditure. After the inspection, most will give you an individualized computer printout that will recommend various energy-saving measures. The printout will also tell you how much these measures are likely to cost and how much each one will save on your annual energy bill.

▶ TURN OFF ELECTRIC STOVE BURNERS EARLY

Your stove is a major user of electric power, so get in the habit of turning off the burners a couple of minutes before the necessary cooking time is up. The heating element on an electric burner stays hot for about that long after it is turned off.

Do the same with either a gas or electric oven. If you don't open the door, an efficient oven will maintain its temperature for five to seven minutes after being turned off.

Have you been in the habit of leaving a pot of food on the burner or in the oven for minutes after turning them off? Now you know why you have been overcooking things.

▶ BOIL WATER IN A CLOSED POT OR KETTLE

It takes twice as long and costs twice as much if you bring water to a boil in an open pot. Don't boil any more water than you need, either. Why fill a teakettle half-full and spend seven minutes' worth of heating time when the ¾ cup you want will come to a boil in three minutes?

▶ USE SMALLER PANS

Use the smallest pans possible; they require less energy.

▶ MATCH THE PAN TO THE BURNER

If you put a 6-inch pan on an 8-inch burner, about 40 percent of the heat produced will be wasted.

▶ KEEP AN INSULATED CARAFE NEXT TO YOUR COFFEE MAKER

After the coffee is made, pour it into a thermos bottle or carafe and turn the electric coffee maker off. You can save a few dollars a year by not using the coffee maker's "keep warm" feature.

▶ BUY A SLOW COOKER

If you often cook foods that require long cooking times, such as casseroles, stews, and soups, using an inexpensive slow cooker like a Crockpot will soon pay for itself.

▶ USE TOASTER OVENS AND MICROWAVES

Use your regular oven only when necessary. Full-size regular ovens use four times as much electricity to accomplish the same cooking task as microwave ovens. Toaster ovens are more efficient, too. But don't use your microwave to boil water; a stove-top burner is more efficient for this task.

▶ SELF-CLEAN OVENS WHILE THEY'RE HOT

If you have a self-cleaning oven, the best time to turn it on is immediately after you've cooked a meal. The oven will still be hot and less energy will be required.

▶ USE A PRESSURE COOKER

Pressure cookers save energy by reducing cooking time by from 25 to 50 percent.

▶ KEEP YOUR FREEZER FULL

Because food retains cold more efficiently than air, a half-empty freezer actually costs more to operate than a full one. If you don't have anything else to put in a freezer, load it up with plastic containers of water.

▶ CLEAN THE CONDENSER COILS ON YOUR REFRIGERATOR

Unfortunately, they're not very conveniently located, so it's easy to forget about them. But you'll never ignore them again after you've watched a $75.00-a-visit service person get your refrigerator back in peak condition simply by vacuuming the condenser coils.

At least once every couple of months, pull your refrigerator away from the wall, unplug it, and vacuum or brush off the coils you'll see on the back of the machine. The dust and dirt that collect there seriously reduce its operating efficiency. If allowed to build up, in fact, the grime can totally block the heat transfer between the coils and the outside air and cause a breakdown of the refrigerator.

When you push the refrigerator back in, make sure that air can circulate freely around the condenser coils. There should be a minimum of 1¼ inches of space between the wall and the refrigerator.

▶ CHECK REFRIGERATOR DOORS

The easiest way to do this is to put a dollar bill in the door when you close it. If the seal on the door doesn't hold the bill firmly in place, it is not working properly. New seals for refrigerators and freezers are not cheap and should be installed by experienced repair people. Before doing so, consider whether you might not be better off buying a new, energy-efficient model (see Chapter 4).

▶ CHECK YOUR REFRIGERATOR'S TEMPERATURE

Don't depend on the settings inside your refrigerator and freezer. Check temperatures with an accurate thermometer every month or so. They should be between 38 and 40 degrees F in the refrigerator and within 1 degree of 0 F, either plus or minus, in the freezer. Keeping a freezer at minus 10 degrees can increase energy use by as much as 20 percent.

▶ COOL AND COVER FOODS BEFORE STORING

Let hot foods cool off before putting them in the refrigerator or freezer, and cover all foods, especially soups and other liquids, to avoid releasing moisture and raising the temperature.

▶ USE WAXED PAPER AND STORAGE CONTAINERS

Washing and saving old aluminum foil (recommended in all those household-hint books) seems to us to be taking penny pinching to extreme limits. Nor do we wash and reuse every plastic bag in which we have stored leftover food. But it is easy to save money by adopting two simple, environmentally friendly ways of storing and cooking food:

- Use waxed paper. Plastic wrap (at least twice as expensive) is better for certain kinds of storage, but biodegradable waxed paper is just as good or even preferable for some food wrapping (sandwiches to be eaten within a couple of hours) and for microwave cooking.

■ Store leftovers in reusable glass or plastic containers. If they are sealed tightly, food will stay fresh longer and you'll cut way back on your use of expensive wraps and disposable bags.

▶ USE COLD WATER WITH YOUR GARBAGE DISPOSAL

Two reasons: Hot water costs extra money, and cold water solidifies grease so it can be ground up by the unit and efficiently washed away.

▶ USE A SPONGE

Too many people habitually use a paper towel every time they clean off a kitchen countertop. That can cost a few more dollars a year than using a sponge.

▶ LET YOUR DISHES AIR-DRY

You can save up to 10 percent of the cost of using your dishwasher with the automatic air-dry switch available on new models. If your unit doesn't have such a switch, you can get the same saving simply by turning off the control knob after the final rinse. Prop the door open a little and the dishes will dry faster.

▶ PRESOAK HEAVILY SOILED CLOTHING

You'll avoid two washings and save energy.

▶ DRY CLOTHES IN CONSECUTIVE LOADS

Stop-and-start drying uses more energy because a lot goes into warming the dryer to the desired temperature each time you begin. Also separate drying loads into heavy and lightweight items; the dryer won't have to stay on as long for the lighter loads.

▶ REMEMBER THE OLD-FASHIONED CLOTHESLINE

A lot of people have forgotten the ultimate energy saver. As a bonus, clothes dried outside often seem fresher than they do when you use an electric or gas dryer.

▶ DO A LIGHT BULB AUDIT OF THE HOUSE

Most Americans overlight their homes. Room by room, analyze how much light is really needed. In many areas of a normal house, such as hallways, basements, and attics, replacing light bulbs with bulbs of lower wattage is an easy way to cut electric bills.

▶ FINALLY! A USE FOR BURNED-OUT LIGHT BULBS

Many older houses are overlit and have fixtures that require two, three, or four bulbs. In nonworking space areas where light can be reduced, put one burned-out bulb in a multiple light fixture. It is safer to have a bulb in a live socket, but the burned-out bulb won't use any electricity.

▶ AVOID LONG-LIFE BULBS

A long-life incandescent bulb in a hard-to-reach place can make sense, but they are less energy efficient than normal bulbs so shouldn't be used generally.

▶ SWITCH TO FLUORESCENT BULBS

New state-of-the-art fluorescent bulbs can save significant amounts of money despite their high initial cost. That's because they use about 75 percent less electricity to produce the same amount of light as incandescent bulbs. They also last ten to thirteen times longer.

Philips produces a fluorescent bulb that uses 18 watts of energy to produce 75 watts of light. Based on a cost of 10 cents per kilowatt hour, the company estimates that its energy-saving bulb will save $57.00 in electric costs over its lifetime. That more than justifies its initial $18.25 price, and you'll also save the cost of ten to thirteen normal 75-watt bulbs.

The new fluorescents produce a much warmer light than the older products and can be used in table lamps. They are much bulkier, though, and there's a time delay of about a second when you turn them on.

You can find a selection of fluorescent bulbs in many lighting stores, or call *The Energy Federation, Inc.* (800-876-0660) for a free catalog. EFI is a nonprofit organization that promotes conservation technologies and products currently difficult to obtain in conventional markets. Its catalog includes energy-efficient lighting products, water conservation products, and weatherization materials. Telephone and mail orders are accepted.

▶ CALL 800-523-2929 WITH ANY ENERGY CONSERVATION QUESTION

This is the number of the Department of Energy's Conservation and Renewable Energy Inquiry and Referral Service (CAREIRS). Your taxes pay for it, but few people seem to realize that information on the full spectrum of renewable energy technologies and energy conservation is available free.

If CAREIRS itself can't answer your questions about such matters as active and passive solar energy, alcohol fuels, wind energy, and the like, they will refer you to appropriate trade or professional associations, federal agencies, or state and local groups.

▶ BUY A BATTERY CHARGER

A nickel-cadmium battery charger with six rechargeable batteries (two each of three sizes) cost $12.99 at our warehouse club last year. A package of two nonrechargeable batteries cost between $1.99 and $2.79 at our hardware store. We expect to save at least $25.00 to $40.00 a year. If you have children who play with lots of battery-operated toys, or if you or teenage children are heavy users of something like a portable cassette player, your savings could easily add up to $200 or more in a year.

▶ DON'T PUT BRICKS IN YOUR TOILET TANK

This often-recommended technique for saving water in older, pre-low-flush toilets usually doesn't work. Chances are, you'll find you often have to flush twice instead of once—an annoyance as well as a waste of water. Better to experiment by lowering the water level an inch or so (just bend the float rod or make a screwdriver adjustment, depending on the type of assembly in the tank). If the toilet still operates efficiently, you'll save a significant amount of water. If not, unbend the float rod a bit until it does.

▶ CHANGE TOOTH-BRUSHING HABITS

Actually, change just one pointless habit shared by millions of people: allowing the water to run while brushing. Wet the brush, turn off the water, apply toothpaste, brush, then turn the water back on to rinse. Savings: in a family of four, each brushing two times a day, from 20,000 to 30,000 gallons of water a year (cost in our area: $25.00–$35.00).

▶ SWITCH TO LOW-FLUSH TOILETS

Since about 1980, most new and remodeled bathrooms have been equipped with "water-conserving" toilets, which typically use about 3.5 gallons per flush instead of the 7 that was the standard for the preceding half a century. In the past couple of years, efficient "low-flush" toilets, which use only 1.6 gallons, have been widely introduced.

Over 35 percent of residential water use in this country is directly attributable to the flushing of toilets, so the environmental benefits of toilets that use less water are compelling. As far as saving money is concerned, especially if you live in an area where water is expensive, replacing a 7-gallon water-waster with a new low-flush toilet will probably pay for itself in from two to five years.

It's easy to work out your own math yourself. *Example:* six flushes a day times 5.4 gallons (7 gallons minus 1.6

gallons) times 350 days a year you are in the house equals 11,340 wasted gallons a year. If you pay $4.00 per thousand gallons of water (check your water bill for your actual cost), that's $45.36 wasted each year. A new toilet will cost $100–$250 plus a plumber's installation charge.

▶ DON'T RENT YOUR TELEPHONE

The cost of buying a basic touch-tone phone is probably not much more than the one-to-two-year cost of renting one from your telephone company. Any well-made telephone should give you years of trouble-free service. And, although it might come as a surprise to some of the millions of people who still rent their telephones from AT&T, on-site repairs are not free anymore. There really is *no* advantage to renting.

If you are still renting, look at your bill. You'll find the number to call to cancel the service and get information about buying your telephone and converting it, if necessary, to a modular instrument (the only kind you want). Check that price against the prices of telephones sold by an electronics discounter (see Chapter 4 for mail-order sources). For guidance on what to look for when you buy, see the next tip.

▶ INSTALL YOUR OWN PHONE

Repair or install new wiring. Pinpoint problems when you have trouble getting a dial tone, the phone doesn't ring, or sound quality is bad. Too difficult? Absolutely not. In fact, modern telephone equipment is easy for even a habitually klutzy do-it-yourselfer to work with.

The single best source of easy-to-understand-and-follow instructions is no further away than your local library, which should have *The Phone Book,* a Consumer Reports Book by Carl Oppendahl. At $15.95, it could be worth your while to own a copy, because this book not only explains how to choose, fix, and install equipment. It is also a virtual encyclopedia of everything you should know about getting the best service at the lowest cost.

▶ READ THE WHITE PAGES OF YOUR TELEPHONE DIRECTORY

Prices and options in telephone service vary greatly in different areas. Different people use their telephones in different ways. So it is impossible to spell out exactly the best penny-pinching strategy for you to use with your local telephone company. But you may very well discover quick and easy ways to save money simply by spending a few minutes reading the first few pages of your telephone directory.

Every detail about different charges, rate time periods, calling plans, etc. must by law be set forth in this directory. Rate structures change frequently, but nobody at your telephone company is going to point out to you that the calling plan you signed up for five years ago may no longer be the least expensive one for you. The directory information will be up-to-date. Match various plans against the usage detailed in your last few telephone bills. For guidance on how to do this, use *The Phone Book* (see previous tip).

▶ STOP PAYING FOR TELEPHONE "WIRE MAINTENANCE"

Pull out your last telephone bill. If you see a charge for wire maintenance (usually from $1.50 to $2.00 a month), call your phone company's business office and cancel this "service." Why? Because you are paying a high premium to insure yourself against an unlikely event.

The phone company is already responsible for maintenance of wires that lead up to your house. The charge on your bill also makes the company responsible for fixing the wires that lead from that point to your telephones. Since problems with inside wires are rare, you are better off taking your chances and paying an electrician (or fixing them yourself; see previous tips) in the unlikely event that something goes wrong.

▶ BUY LONG-DISTANCE SERVICE THAT FITS YOUR USER PROFILE

Fierce competition among long-distance telephone companies has resulted in a competitive stand-off in terms of most regular rates for most users. All the companies offer discount plans for different kinds of usage, however, and it is possible to cut your bills substantially using one of them.

Which plan? Which company? Those aren't the right first questions. The single best penny-pincher strategy is first to analyze how you and your family actually use long-distance service and only then look into different discount plans. If you make just a few short calls a month, a discount plan offering a flat rate for the first one hour of service may not make sense. If you make most of your calls to a single area code, you may want to take advantage of a discount plan that makes that cheaper.

Unless you can find a new plan that would have saved you money based on your analysis of a few months' worth of long-distance bills, don't switch from your present carrier. One common mistake is to buy a plan that offers steep discounts with a minimum fee for late night use, based on a vow to change your habits by talking to your sister on the other coast only after 10:00 P.M. After an initial period of compliance, you will probably fall back into old routines and end up paying a minimum fee for an unused service.

It's a good idea to look into competitive plans whenever your long-distance calling habits change—when a child goes away to college, for instance, or when a close friend moves. Don't sign a long-term contract (more than six months) with any long-distance company, no matter what promotional advantages are offered. And don't sign up with any carrier because they promise rebates stretching into the far future. Reason: none of them will guarantee their rates won't change, and the rebates—or the terms of your long-term contract—may not look so attractive in a few months. You have a legal right to switch long-distance carriers whenever you like, so keep them competing for your business.

When you do decide to switch, make sure to ask your

new long-distance carrier to credit you for the switching fee (currently $5.00 in our area) charged by your local telephone company. Also, watch your bills carefully during the following ninety days; your old carrier may conveniently neglect to drop you and still bill you for some kind of monthly fee.

Four numbers to call for up-to-date information on available discount plans: *AT&T* (800-222-0300); *MCI* (800-444-3333); *US Sprint* (800-877-4646); *Allnet* (800-631-4000). Or, if you prefer a single source that gives you comprehensive listings and comparisons of various long-distance plans currently available, send $2.00 with SASE to TRAC (*Telecommunications Research & Action Center*), Box 12038, Washington, D.C. 20005.

▶ AVOID YOUR HOTEL'S LONG-DISTANCE LINE

If you don't yet have one, get your own long-distance charge card from AT&T, US Sprint, MCI, or other carrier, and place your calls through its operator. Whether it is a great luxury hotel in a major city or a budget motel out in the sticks, long-distance calls by guests are often looked upon as a source of incremental profits. Surcharges of 100 percent or more are common.

If you are traveling abroad, things are even worse. But MCI (800-444-4444 for information), US Sprint (800-877-4646), and AT&T (USA Direct information, 800-874-4000) have toll-free access numbers abroad that connect you with an operator in the United States. Not only will you save money; you'll also avoid non-English-speaking operators.

▶ BEWARE OF PAY PHONES

One of the best reasons to carry a telephone card from one of the major long-distance companies is to use the access number on it when you are in a pay phone. When you dial this access number, you'll be connected to your carrier's operator and will pay its rates for calling-card or collect calls. Otherwise, if you are unlucky enough to be calling from a pay phone owned by a company that pays a commission to the owners of the facility in which the phone is placed, you risk paying up to five times as much for your call.

▶ GET THE BEST DEAL IN A CALLING CARD

Calling-card rates are invariably higher than the rates you pay when you call from your home phone. But long-distance companies usually offer special discounts on calls made with calling cards issued to home subscribers ("primary users" to the carriers). If you make frequent calls with a card, factor this into your decision about a long-distance carrier.

▶ GET YOUR OWN 800 NUMBER

This could make sense if someone in the family travels a great deal, you have kids away at college, or there are other reasons why you pay for hours of long-distance calls made each month to your home number. For a low monthly fee (MCI and Allnet charge from $5.00 to $10.00 a month, and competition keeps prices from all the long-distance carriers within a narrow range), you can own your own 800 number. Calls to it will cost (again, MCI and Allnet current rates) from 22 to 25 cents a minute—cheaper than calling-card rates from most distances. You don't need any new equipment and don't even have to pay a connection fee; calls come in on your present line. You also have complete control over who knows about the 800 number.

For information and current rates, call the numbers listed in the previous tip about buying long-distance service. Ask for details about a personal 800 number.

▶ USE THE PHONE BOOK

Phone companies have turned their directory-assistance operations into major profit centers. In our area, it costs 48 cents to get an in-state number from an operator. How much longer does it take to look a number up yourself?

▶ USE CHEAP BUT GOOD SUBSTITUTES: BAKING SODA

It is hard for many people to accept, but a lot of brand name products are no better at certain tasks than some simple, cheap alternatives that our great-grandparents knew about. In many cases, the only active ingredient in the brand name products *is* the alternative; what you pay dearly for are things like fragrances, fancy packages, and brand images.

This is not to say that, because plain baking soda has a multitude of possible uses, it is as effective in all of them as any brand name product. It isn't. Until the introduction of fluoride toothpaste, a good case could be made that baking soda was as effective a dentifrice as anything else. It no longer is.

What follows, then, is not a complete catalog of all the ways you might use baking soda. But we believe baking soda is still superior to, or at least equally as effective as, branded products for these uses:

- *As a carpet deodorizer.* Sprinkle it on a dry carpet, brush it in a bit, leave for at least an hour, then vacuum.
- *To remove odors from refrigerators and freezers.* Keep an open box in your refrigerator as a preventative.
- *To clean and deodorize thermos bottles, coffeepots, etc.* Use it just as you would any cleaning powder.
- *As a general scouring powder.* Baking soda is an effective cleaning agent for pots and pans, stove tops, etc. Good on porcelain because it is less abrasive than other scouring powders.
- *As a toilet bowl cleaner.*
- *As an antacid.* If you are on a low-sodium diet or have other medical reasons to avoid sodium bicarbonate (baking soda), check with your doctor first. But sodium bicarbonate is the only active ingredient in many brand name antacids sold for twenty or thirty times what it will cost you by the teaspooon out of a plain baking soda box. Just add a teaspoon to a 6-ounce glass of water.
- *As a fire extinguisher.* Keep a box next to the stove to use in case of a small grease fire. Water won't work on a grease fire and will probably make it worse.

Want more? The Arm & Hammer Company offers a free wheel guide to other uses of baking soda. Send your name and address to Arm & Hammer Wheel Offer, Box 4533, Department E, Monticello, MN 55365.

▶ USE CHEAP BUT GOOD SUBSTITUTES: WHITE VINEGAR

White vinegar is just as good or better than brand name products for these uses:

- *To scour copper pans.* Mix ½ tablespoon salt with ¼ cup of vinegar. Scrub on, remove with water, then wipe dry to shine.
- *To clean and shine chromium faucets.* Wipe on, wipe off with a paper towel.
- *To remove coffee oil residue.* Once a week, soak and then scrub the filter holder of your coffee maker with vinegar diluted in an equal amount of water. You can also use a vinegar–water mix in your automatic coffee maker, turning it on after you insert a clean filter. After all of the vinegar solution has come through, repeat the process using plain water to rinse.
- *To remove soap residue* from clothing, add a half cup of vinegar to your washer's last rinse cycle. This is safe for most fabrics and will also eliminate static cling.

▶ USE CHEAP BUT GOOD SUBSTITUTES: MINERAL OIL

- *Instead of baby oil.* Actually, baby oil *is* mineral oil plus a fragrance.
- *To remove eye makeup.* Read the ingredients on your current brand's package. Mineral oil is the only active ingredient.

▶ USE CHEAP BUT GOOD SUBSTITUTES: CORNSTARCH

- *Instead of talcum powder.* It is at least ten times as absorbent, and it is pure enough to use as a baby powder.

- *As a carpet cleaner.* Probably not as effective on hard-to-remove stains as some other products, but an effective absorbent powder for general use and safe on any fabric. Brush it on, leave for at least an hour, then vacuum. Mix 1 cup of cornstarch with 2 tablespoons of ground cloves and 2 cups of baking soda to deodorize as well as clean carpets. Leave on overnight before vacuuming.
- *For grease stains.* Shake on, let dry, brush off.
- *After polishing furniture* with furniture oil, sprinkle on a little cornstarch and wipe off. It will absorb oil and help maintain a finger-proof surface.

▶ MAKE YOUR OWN WINDOW-CLEANING FLUID

There are a number of cheap alternatives to the expensive blue stuff inside that fancy brand name spray bottle. Save the pump sprayer and the bottle, but when it is empty fill it instead with:

- 2 ounces household ammonia mixed with one quart of water. Good for most jobs. If you miss the color of the expensive stuff, add a drop of blue food coloring; it won't do any harm.
- 2 ounces household ammonia, 4 ounces rubbing alcohol, and half a teaspoon of dishwater detergent mixed with one quart of water. Helps keep windows frost free.
- 1 ounce of deodorized kerosene mixed with a quart of water is particularly effective on extremely dirty, greasy windows.

To avoid streaking, don't wash windows when they are in direct sunlight. All cleaners can damage painted surfaces; wash them off quickly with plain water and dry. Using old newspapers is cheap but messy; we prefer paper towels.

▶ FREEZE CANDLES BEFORE USING

Not only will they burn more slowly, saving money, candles will also burn more evenly and with minimal wax dripping if you put them in the freezer for a few hours before lighting.

▶ PLUMBING: QUICK AND EASY FIXES

- *For running toilets.* The odds are that all you need is a new flapper or tank ball. Turn off the water valve under the toilet, take the tank cover off, and unscrew the ball or (in newer assemblies) lift off the flapper. Buy a new one ($3.00 to $6.00), install (it will come with instructions, but essentially you are just reversing the procedure by which you removed the old one), and turn the water back on. If the toilet still runs, check out other possible solutions in a good do-it-yourself repair book.
- *For clogged drains.* Try a plunger first. It will usually work. You can avoid most clogged drains in kitchen sinks, usually the result of grease deposits, by pouring a half cup of baking soda and a half cup of vinegar down the drain once a month. Wait fifteen minutes, then flush with hot water.
- *For obstructed showerheads.* Unscrew, soak in a half and half solution of vinegar and water, then remove sediment using a small brush. If this doesn't work, buy and install a new one.

▶ APPLIANCES AND ELECTRIC CORDS: QUICK AND EASY FIXES

- *For defective electric stove burners.* Turn off the stove, pull up the burner, and unplug it from its outlet. Do the same thing with a working burner of the same size. Replace the defective burner with the working burner. Turn it on. If it works now, all you have to do is buy a replacement at an appliance store. If it doesn't, call the repair service.
- *For clothes dryers that won't heat.* It is embarrassing to call in an expert to clean lint from the filter inside the dryer or the one you'll find in the venting pipe. That's often the only problem, though.

■ *For loose or damaged electric plugs.* There is a wonderful new snap-on plug for sale in hardware stores for about $3.00. All you have to do is cut the old plug off the cord, push the cord into the new plug, and snap it shut. No involved knot-tying and handling of wires is necessary. The snap-on plug works on the kind of flat cord used with most lamps and appliances.

▶ DOORS: QUICK AND EASY FIXES

■ *For stuck door locks.* Buy a tube of graphite at the hardware store and squirt it into the keyhole. Work it in by turning the key a few times.

■ *For doors that won't latch.* First check the hinges and tighten loose ones with a screwdriver. If that alone doesn't solve the problem, put some colored chalk on the latch bolt, close the door, and see how far from the hole in the strike plate it hits. Usually the difference is so slight that you can tap the top or bottom edge of the strike plate with a small hammer, enlarging the hole enough to allow the bolt to engage.

■ *For doors that won't slide.* Clean and wipe the tracks of the sliding door assembly. Then spray with a high viscosity silicone product such as It or, in a pinch, rub the tracks down with a bar of soap.

▶ WATER YOUR GARDEN AND LAWN AT NIGHT

At noon on a sunny summer day, probably half the water a lawn sprinkler throws on your lawn evaporates before it does any good. If you water at night, you can cut back significantly on the amount used. Your grass, flowers, and shrubs won't know the difference.

▶ GET THE MOST FOR YOUR FERTILIZER DOLLAR

A 25-pound bag of fertilizer for $20.00 may not be a better buy than another at $25.00. The easiest way to judge is by nitrogen content; a higher count is worth more.

▶ PLANT DECIDUOUS TREES TO THE SOUTH AND WEST

Trees and vines that lose their leaves in the winter can cut your costs of heating and cooling significantly. Plant them on the south and west sides of your house; they will provide shade in the summer but allow sunshine in in the winter.

▶ TRY A PUSH LAWN MOWER

Unless you live on a third of an acre or more, it won't take much more effort or time to use a nonpower push lawn mower instead of a smoky gas guzzler. Most people are surprised at how little effort is needed to push one of the well-made new models. You'll cut your annual mower maintenance bills by at least 300 percent (a bit of lubricating oil and an occasional blade sharpening will do it), save on gas, save at least 100 percent on the initial price of the mower, and reduce air pollution. And most of us can use the extra exercise.

▶ CHECK INTO YOUR PROPERTY TAXES

It takes very little time, and a surprising percentage of home owners who look at their "property record card" at their tax assessor's office find errors. The card may record the wrong lot size or list a nonexistent bedroom, for instance. If so, you have immediate cause for an appeal that could cut your property tax bill.

Even if there's no mistake on the card, but you believe that comparable houses in your area are assessed at a lower rate, you may be able to win an appeal. A local real estate agent can verify your suspicions and probably even give you some advice on the best way to state your case in a formal appeal. For a fee (usually half of whatever you save in the first year after a successful appeal), you can hire an independent consultant (see "tax consultants" in the Yellow Pages) to do all the work for you. Get references before you hire such a consultant, since anyone can claim to be an expert in this unlicensed field.

3

Reducing Insurance Premiums and Taxes

Twenty-five years before he uttered the immortal phrase, "Nothing is certain but death and taxes," Benjamin Franklin started America's first insurance company. Obviously he still had no idea how inevitable a part of our lives insurance premiums would become.

That very inevitability leads some people to treat their insurance bills, along with taxes, as fixed and unalterable. They wince when they get their semiannual automobile insurance premium bill and see that the premium has gone up once again. But they decide it is easier to pay the bill than to open up that boring file filled with years' worth of unexamined policies, policy changes, and premium notices.

It's easy for these people to make two basic mistakes about insurance. They pay more than they should for the insurance they have, often because they don't really need all of it. And they don't insure or grossly underinsure themselves against some very real risks.

47

Insurance of any kind is simply a way for a large group of people (the policyholders of an insurance company) to *share risk*. There's only a small risk of your house being one of the few thousand in the country that will burn to the ground in the next year, but if that did happen it would be a financial catastrophe for you. So you pay a small amount each year to protect yourself against that loss. You *want* what you pay for insurance premiums to be "a waste of money."

Cheap is not always the best penny-pinching idea when it comes to insurance. Although there may be some governmental or industry safety nets in place to protect you in case your insurance company goes bankrupt, you certainly don't want to test them. Deal only with insurance companies rated A or A+ for financial stability in *Best's Insurance Reports,* published by the A.M. Best Company and available in most libraries.

Only after you have established that the companies you are considering are financially sound should you begin comparison shopping among them. Price now becomes a compelling factor, but so is service; talk to people who have dealt with the company when a claim was necessary. Don't avoid paying a bit more if it will give you access to a knowledgeable agent who is willing to tailor a program that is right for your individual needs.

Finally, keep in mind that too many insurance agents love customers whose eyes glaze over because all the details are confusing and the whole subject is, well, *dull.* You can't afford to feel that way about your money and your family's security.

As for taxes, Ben Franklin has yet to be proven wrong. But simply because taxes are inevitable doesn't mean you shouldn't do everything legally possible to minimize them.

This book is not an income-tax guide. But many readers of tax preparation guides who are concentrating on line-by-line instructions for their returns are likely to miss the penny-pinching strategies included in this chapter. These strategies may also require you to analyze your tax situation well before the end of a calendar year. If you wait until next April, it is often too late to activate some very easy ways to reduce this year's—or next year's—taxes.

▶ BUY THE HIGHEST POSSIBLE DEDUCTIBLES

Whether you are buying automobile, home, or medical insurance, the purpose of insurance is to protect against sudden, unforeseen expenses that you could not afford yourself. If a leaky pipe were to cause $300 worth of damage to a ceiling, for instance, spending that sum might be frustrating, even painful. But if you can afford it, you shouldn't insure yourself against it by paying for a homeowner's policy with a $100 deductible.

Such a policy would pay for $200 of the damages in this case. But the premium paid for a policy with that low a deductible will be much more expensive than one with a $500 deductible. The lower your deductibles (the amount over which your insurance company has to pay the damages), the higher your insurance premiums. The difference in premium cost betweeen a $500 and a $100 deductible for your home or car can be 30 percent or even more.

There's another practical reason to buy the highest possible deductibles for auto and home insurance. Many insurance companies punish people who file too many claims by raising their premiums. In fact, just a couple of small claims may be too many for some companies. If you are therefore going to limit your claims to large amounts of money, it would be extra foolish to pay for low deductibles at the same time.

▶ BUT DON'T UNDERINSURE

The big risks are the ones you are worried about. If you have a car that's less than three or four years old, don't try to save on auto insurance by skipping collision coverage. If your family would need $200,000 to live decently and you could no longer provide for them, don't try to get away with a smaller life insurance policy. If you live in a house that would cost $150,000 to replace if it burned to the ground, don't settle for anything less than a homeowner's policy that guarantees full replacement cost.

Pinching pennies doesn't mean being pound foolish; the worst way to save money is by risking future financial catastrophe.

▶ KNOW HOW MUCH LIFE INSURANCE YOU NEED

How much you need is more important than what kind you buy. So you must calculate what your family would need to replace you—financially—if you died tomorrow.

There are a bewildering number of different kinds of life insurance policies. But the first basic choice you must make is between term insurance, which pays off only if you die, and one of the many forms of permanent insurance, which also pays the amount of the policy in case you die but in addition is worth something while you are alive. As the agents say, it has both insurance and investment components.

You'll pay less for term insurance. Many parents use a combination of term and permanent insurance during the years before their children are self-sufficient, then drop the term insurance. You'll have to spend some time in your library and with life insurance agents before you decide what's best for you. Just one word of advice: Take with a grain of salt the arguments of both the "buy-only-term-and-invest-the-rest" crowd and the "term-is-a-waste-of-money" school. There is no answer that fits everyone, and many people are best off with a combination of both.

Back to the big question: How much will you need? Start with the worksheet on page 51; it will be a big help if you fill it out before reading books and talking to agents. Actually, this is a simplified version of the capital needs analysis form a good agent will use.

Because it is easier to use such a worksheet if you can see how it applies in a real life example, we've included a column with numbers filled in. Our example is a man of thirty, married, with an income of $50,000 a year. His wife works part time, making $12,000 a year, and they have a two-year-old child. The man has a $100,000 group life insurance policy through his job. They have just moved into a $150,000 house, using all but $10,000 of their total joint savings for a down payment of $30,000.

The example covers this man's life insurance needs only; his wife's should be calculated separately. Note that he needs assets of $318,000 to pay off the mortgage on

How Much Life Insurance Do You Need?

To Cover:	What they'll need	Example
1. Funeral		$ 3,000
2. Other miscellaneous final expenses	+	+ $ 1,000
3. Estate taxes	+	+ 0
4. Pay off mortgage	+	+ $120,000
5. Pay off other debts	+	+ $ 1,000
6. College fund	+	+ $ 44,000
7. Other needs	+	+ $ 5,000
8. Total	=	$174,000
Living expenses:		
Current living expenses		$ 45,000
× 80 percent		$ 36,000
− Spouse's take home pay	−	$ 12,000
− Social Security survivor benefit	−	$ 16,000
= Annual need	=	$ 7,200
× number of years needed		20
9. Total living expenses	=	$144,000
10. Total assets needed (add 8 + 9)		$318,000
11. Group insurance proceeds	−	$100,000
12. Income producing assets	−	$ 10,000
13. Your insurance need (10 − 11 + 12)		$208,000

the house and other debts, send his child to college, and cover twenty years of living expenses for his wife and child. In this case, he and his wife decided that she and the child could both be self-supporting after the child graduates from college. Since he already has a $100,000 group policy and $10,000 in assets that could provide income, his insurance need comes to $208,000.

Not many thirty-year-olds making $50,000 a year will be able to afford that much permanent life insurance, so some combination of term and permanent is likely.

The worksheet doesn't take inflation into account, although investing the insurance proceeds wisely should keep pace with inflation. There are no taxes on estates of less than $600,000. Your family might not choose to pay off your mortgage and other debt, but doing so simplifies the necessary calculations.

Adjust up or down our estimate of 80 percent of current living expenses as the amount your family could live on. *Don't* use the Social Security Survivor Benefit number in the example. Write or call the Social Security Administration (Box 4429, Albuquerque, NM 87196; 800-937-7005) and ask for a Request for Personal Benefits Estimate Statement; you'll eventually get an estimate of your own current survivor's benefits. And by all means, adapt or add to this basic worksheet in any way necessary to fit your individual needs.

▶ SHOP FOR TERM INSURANCE BY TELEPHONE

It's an easy way to check out rates and compare them with what your own agent or bank has offered. There is no fee involved; just call one of the clearinghouse companies below and tell them how much coverage you want. They'll ask your age, what the general state of your health is, and other pertinent questions. A couple of weeks later you'll receive a free computer printout listing prices from several companies. Before you buy, check the company out in *Best's* (see page 48) and make sure you understand all the terms of the contract. Companies to call:

- *Select Quote*, 800-343-1985
- *Term Quote*, 800-444-TERM

▶ SKIP LIFE INSURANCE FOR CHILDREN

Your kids won't need life insurance until they have dependents. Insurance cushions you only against financial losses, not emotional ones.

► GROUP RATES AREN'T ALWAYS BETTER

Many companies pay the premiums on employee life insurance policies. Obviously, this is a great deal. Many also allow you to buy additional life insurance at group rates. This *isn't* always a good deal. First, because you may not have the right to convert to an individual policy if you leave the company. Second, because "group rates" for this kind of insurance aren't necessarily less expensive than a term policy you could buy on your own. Comparison-shop before you sign up.

Exception: If you are in poor health, you should probably grab any group rate policy you can get, since you won't have to take a medical exam to get the insurance.

► SAVE ON DISABILITY INSURANCE

Don't save by skimping on it. Disability insurance, which provides ongoing monthly income if you are physically unable to work due to accident or illness, is essential if you have to work to maintain your life-style. That includes most of the nonretired population, but too many people believe Social Security and Workman's Compensation laws provide adequate protection. They don't. Since one of every seven workers in the United States will suffer a five-year or longer period of disability before age sixty-five, a good disability policy is just as important as a good life insurance program.

Most people are covered by group disability insurance where they work. More and more often, they must choose from among different features within flexible benefit plans. If you aren't covered by a group plan, you will have to pay higher individual rates. In either case, the best way to save on premiums without skimping on necessary coverage is to choose a longer waiting period. A thirty-day waiting period—the time between the onset of a disability and when benefits start—is more expensive than a ninety-day waiting period. If you have a reasonable emergency fund, you won't absolutely need the money and you'll save a significant amount in premiums.

▶ HAVE FLEXIBLE BENEFITS? PAY YOUR OWN DISABILITY PREMIUM

More companies each year are offering flexible benefit plans, allowing employees to choose from a smorgasbord of health, life, and disability plans but limiting the company's total contribution to premium payments. It makes sense to have the company pay the non-disability premiums first. If there's none of their money left over, buy your own disability insurance through the company's low group rate. Why? If the company pays disability premiums, and someday you need to collect benefits, payments would be taxable to you as ordinary income. If you pay the premiums, payments would be tax-free.

▶ THE PENNY-PINCHER'S DOWNFALL: MEDICAL INSURANCE

The fact that the United States is confronting a crisis in health care costs has been well documented elsewhere. Even if the cost of your group benefits through your employer has doubled or tripled in the past couple of years, count yourself lucky if you still have comprehensive major medical insurance. More than 40 million Americans have no medical insurance at all, and people with individual policies are paying as much as $8,000 to $10,000 a year.

We have no advice about how to cut those costs and still retain the benefits most people want. You simply have to give up something to reduce premiums. Higher deductibles are one alternative. Right now, your policy may pay 80 percent of your medical bills after you pay the first $250 each year, and 100 percent after those bills total $5,000. If everyone in your family is in good health and you seldom visit a doctor or take medicines or drugs, you might want to raise your annual deductible from $250 to $2,500. If a policy like that is available, you would still have insurance against a medical catastrophe, and your premium costs would be significantly lower.

You should also consider Health Maintenance Organizations (HMOs) and/or Preferred Provider Organizations (PPOs). Many employers have changed their benefit plans in such a way that employees have little choice but to join an HMO. The good ones provide excellent medical care at a lower cost than traditional medical providers, but you will be limited to doctors and hospitals within the HMO organization.

▶ SHOP FOR AUTO INSURANCE BY TELEPHONE

The next time you get the premium bill for your auto insurance, take a few minutes to do some comparison shopping. It really isn't much trouble when you do it by telephone, and the results may surprise you. If nothing else, you can satisfy yourself that the rates you are paying are competitive. Ask friends who they use and how satisfied they have been; among the companies you might try are USAA, State Farm, GEICO, and Allstate.

Most insurance companies will quote prices by telephone. Even those who at first say they won't may change their minds when you tell them it's the only way you'll do business. Enter the information they'll need from you along with the prices from your current policy in the worksheet on pages 58–59. Don't volunteer any information they don't need, but be honest about mileage, moving violations, etc.

Establish all of your current deductibles and get prices based on those. If you want to explore different deductibles, make sure you get a quote from your current company as well as the competition.

It's possible other companies may offer discounts your present company doesn't. Ask. There may be others in addition to those listed at the bottom of the worksheet.

▶ DROP COLLISION INSURANCE ON OLDER CARS

Especially if you follow our penny-pinching advice on buying high deductibles, it doesn't make sense to pay for collision insurance on a car that is worth less than $2,500. If you have a $500 deductible, the most you could collect would be $2,000. Your collision premium for that maximum coverage could be from $100 to $200 a year—5 to 10 percent of your highest possible claim. That's far too high a price to pay for the risk involved.

▶ SAVE ON HOMEOWNER'S INSURANCE

Homeowner's insurance is easier to buy than some other types because the industry has a standard coding system (the HO number) that identifies different types of policies. Many policies also label themselves as "comprehensive" or "all-risk," but these are meaningless terms. The HO number tells you what you are buying.

HO-1, HO-2, HO-3, and HO-5 policies are for house owners. An HO-6 policy is for owners of condominiums or co-ops. An HO-4 policy is for renters who need coverage for the contents of their houses or apartments as well as the same kind of personal liability insurance (in case someone is injured on the premises) homeowner policies provide.

If you are a homeowner, avoid the HO-1 and HO-2 policies, which are too limited to provide adequate protection, and price out HO-3 ("open peril") and HO-5 ("comprehensive, all-risk") policies. The HO-5 is more expensive because, although it has the same coverage as the HO-3 on the structure, it offers broader coverage on contents. Most people find the extra coverage isn't worth the increase in premium payments.

Perhaps the most important feature you should insist on (and pay extra for) in an HO-3 policy is guaranteed replacement. This means that if you insure your house for 100 percent of its value as determined by the insurance company, they will rebuild it no matter what that costs, even if the cost exceeds the amount of the policy.

Among the ways to save on homeowner's insurance:

- Install smoke alarms.
- Consider some form of anti-theft system, but don't install an expensive system just to save on insurance premiums. Depending on where you live, the savings may not be very large.

- Get nonsmoker's discounts if you qualify.
- Use the same company for your automobile policy, and get a combination policy discount.
- Shop around. For most people, automobile insurance is more expensive than homeowner's insurance, so you may want to price that out first. But look at the total costs of both from different companies. Most of the companies mentioned in the tip about auto insurance also sell homeowner's, and you should also talk to at least one independent agent in your area.
- HO-4 (renter's) policies vary widely in price, particularly in major metropolitan areas with higher-than-average burglary statistics. It is especially important to get estimates from a number of different insurers, compare exactly what is covered in each policy, and weigh the premium costs of different levels of deductibles.

▶ AVOID CREDIT INSURANCE

Most credit-granting organizations (banks, auto dealers, etc.) will attempt to sell credit life and/or disability insurance to you in connection with the loans they make. It is hardly ever a good idea. If you need more life insurance, a separate term policy sold by the bank or an insurance agent will always be cheaper. What's more, if you buy credit insurance, the beneficiary is not your family, but the lender. That's not who you want to protect in case of your death or disability.

▶ ONE FAIL-SAFE WAY TO SAVE ON CAR INSURANCE

Most states now mandate a certain percentage discount in car insurance premiums for anyone who has recently taken a defensive driving course. Admittedly, there's a trade-off of time here—the courses typically run six to eight hours in two evening sessions—but the savings can be major (as much as $150 a year), recurring (for three to five years), and you get an important dividend: You may just learn something that could help you avoid an accident.

Comparing Automobile Insurance: A Worksheet

A. List cars you plan to insure:

  Car A: Year, model, vehicle i.d. number ......

    Miles driven per year ....

    Percentage used for commuting ....

  Car B: Year, model, vehicle i.d. number ......

    Miles driven per year ....

    Percentage used for commuting ....

B. List members of family who use the cars:
Include name, age, driver's license number,
convictions for moving violations and dates,
accident records, percentage of use on each car

C. Comparing premiums:

	CURRENT POLICY		CO.		CO.		CO.	
	Car 1	Car 2	Car 1	Car 2	Car 1	Car 2	Car 1	Car 2
1. Bodily injury liability: $_____ per person $_____ per occurrence								
2. Property damage liability: $_____ per occurrence								
3. Medical payments: $_____ (Note terms/deductibles, etc.)								

4. No-fault personal injury protection:

$ _____

5. Uninsured motorists:

$ _____ / _____ bodily injury person/occurrence

6. Auto medical payments:

$ _____ each person

7. Collision:

$ _____ deductible
$ _____ deductible
$ _____ deductible

8. Comprehensive:

$ _____ deductible
$ _____ deductible
$ _____ deductible

9. Discounts:

_____ % of _____ for air bags/automatic belts
_____ % of _____ for anti-theft devices
_____ % of _____ for safe-driver education
_____ % of _____ for senior drivers
_____ % of _____ for _____
_____ % of _____ for _____

TOTAL COSTS (total using deductibles selected
less applicable discounts): _____

▶ SKIP AIR TRAVEL INSURANCE

Don't buy it at the airport, and don't buy it from the credit card company that makes it "so easy," after you allow them automatically to add a "small" charge for $100,000 worth of insurance whenever you use the card to buy your tickets.

That "small" charge is actually a ridiculously high insurance premium, given the statistics on airline fatalities. If your dependents need protection, they need it whether you die in an airplane crash or from a heart attack. For the same reason, and because premiums are similarly overpriced, never buy illness-specific life insurance either.

▶ SKIP CAR RENTAL INSURANCE

You can't unless you are already covered, of course, but most people are. Most personal automobile insurance policies cover you for damage to a rental car. Many credit card companies also now offer free car rental insurance as a way to persuade you to use their card. If the credit card companies can afford to give it away free, think how profitable selling the insurance must be for the rental car companies.

▶ SKIP CONTACT LENS INSURANCE

Unless you constantly lose your lenses, the cost of the annual premium plus the deductibles we've seen make this kind of insurance another consumer ripoff.

▶ SKIP STUDENT ACCIDENT INSURANCE

If you have family health-insurance coverage, you don't need this coverage, which is offered by many school districts. They like selling these policies because the district is less likely to be sued by a purchaser in case of an accident.

▶ REVIEW LIFE INSURANCE NEEDS AS YOU GET OLDER

When you have been paying life insurance premiums regularly for a number of years, it is easy to lose sight of just why you bought the insurance in the first place. Most people do so to protect their families in case of loss of income. As you get older, put kids through college, and, hopefully, build a good retirement fund and substantial other assets, you may not need life insurance at all.

Certainly, once you have retired, your family doesn't need protection from loss of your income. In fact, your spouse's expenses would be reduced if you die. Paying larger and larger premiums for renewable term insurance makes no sense at all for many older people.

▶ PREPARE YOUR OWN TAX RETURNS

Given the starting point of 2 percent of adjusted gross income for all miscellaneous deductions, most of us can no longer deduct the cost of an outside tax preparer on our income-tax returns. Fortunately, especially if you have access to a personal computer, you can now safely dispense with outside experts unless you are in the tiny minority of people who have extraordinarily complicated tax problems.

There are at least four very good tax-preparation software programs. We use *TaxCut*, published by MECA (less than $80.00 at discount software retailers), which also publishes the best personal financial management software program, Andrew Tobias's *Managing Your Money*. The great thing about *TaxCut* is that you simply answer simple, direct questions—the same ones an accountant would ask you—and the program does the rest. The program audits and double-checks everything, points out possible discrepancies and omissions, and, only when you are 100 percent sure of yourself, prints out complete forms that can be mailed to the IRS.

If you don't have a personal computer, there are a number of annual income tax guides such as *J. K. Lasser's*

Your Income Tax Guide (Prentice Hall) and Ernst & Young's *Arthur Young Tax Guide* (Ballantine) that are reliable if somewhat more difficult and time-consuming to use.

▶ BEGIN DECEMBER WITH A TAX STRATEGY SESSION

Too many people put off thinking about income taxes until March or April, when the forms are due. By that time it is too late to take advantage of a few simple techniques that can transfer income and/or expenses from one year to another.

Suppose you are reading this in late 1993, and know roughly what your final income will be for that year. If you expect your income, tax rates, and/or tax brackets to be lower in 1994, you have got a good reason to 1) defer as much potential 1993 income as possible to 1994, and 2) move as many deductions as possible from 1994 to 1993.

If it looks like your 1994 taxes will be higher than 1993's, on the other hand, you will probably want to 1) move as much potential 1994 income into 1993 as possible, and 2) defer deductions from 1993 to 1994.

The next two tips tell you a few ways to do both.

▶ PAY LOWER TAXES THIS YEAR

It is December 1993 and you think your potential taxes will be lower for calendar year 1994 than for calendar year 1993. Consider doing the following:

- Look ahead at the charitable contributions you would normally make in 1994. Write those checks, and mail them, on the last day of 1993.
- Prepay real-estate taxes. If a property-tax bill is due in January, pay it instead in December.
- Prepay state and local income taxes. Even if they're not due until April, if you pay in December you can deduct them on your 1993 federal return. Pay all outstanding estimated state taxes in December.
- Prepay your mortgage payment. Make your January

payment on December 31 instead, and deduct that month's mortgage interest from your 1993 return.

- Look over medical expenses for the year. If your total medical expenses (including insurance premiums, doctors, dentists, hospitals, drugs, eyeglasses, contact lenses, hearing aids, and medically necessary travel) amount to 7.5 percent of your adjusted gross income (AGI), you can deduct expenses that exceed that threshold. This would make December 1993 a great time for any kind of elective medical or dental care you know you'll need sooner or later.
- Defer bonuses. This is a bit tricky, and you should get the advice of a tax expert, but if you have been getting a regular bonus at the end of December and can change that on a permanent basis to January, you should be able to defer your tax liability as well.
- Buy CDs and Treasury bills that mature next year. You are not credited with the interest on either until they mature. Actually, if you are trying to reduce interest income for the year, doing this in December doesn't help much. If, however, back in July you had bought a six-month CD maturing in January 1994, you could have deferred quite a bit of interest income. Tax planning is really a year-round activity.
- If you want to take a capital gain, postpone the sale until January 2.
- If self-employed, bill clients in early January instead of late December.

▶ PAY LOWER TAXES NEXT YEAR

It is December 1993 and you think your potential taxes will be higher for calendar year 1994 than they have been for calendar year 1993. Consider doing the following:

- If you normally get a bonus in January, ask if you can instead get it on the last workday of 1993.
- If you normally make charitable contributions at the end of the year, write the checks instead on January 2.
- Delay payment of medical and dental bills until 1994.

- If you have been thinking about selling assets for a capital gain, you have an extra reason to sell now instead of next year.
- Cash in CDs that would mature in 1994, or ask your bank to credit the interest on them by the end of 1993.
- Cash in savings bonds before the end of the year. Especially if your income in 1993 was considerably lower than you think it will be for the next few years, you have a good reason to cash in savings bonds that may have accumulated years of accrued interest income.

▶ DON'T BUY SHARES IN A STOCK MUTUAL FUND IN EARLY DECEMBER

Unless you have other good reasons to do so (dollar cost averaging being one of them), you are probably better off waiting until the very end of December or January 2 of the new year to buy shares in a stock mutual fund. The reason: These funds usually make their capital-gain as well as major income distributions for the year in mid-December. You incur a tax liability for that year on whatever amounts are distributed to you (even if you take the distributions in the form of more shares in the fund).

This is no reason to avoid a stock mutual fund you want to invest in for the long term, but toward the end of the year you should at least call the fund's customer service department to check on when a distribution will be made.

▶ TAKE CAPITAL GAINS EARLY IN THE YEAR

Don't make any investment decisions based solely on tax consequences. All else being equal, though, the earlier in the year you take a capital gain, the longer a period of time you have to put that gain to work before paying taxes in April of next year. If you will pay a 28 percent tax on the gain but invest it for a full year in a mutual fund that gains 14 percent, the tax hurts 50 percent less.

▶ SHIFT INCOME TO YOUR KIDS

A dependent child under fourteen can receive up to $500

unearned income (dividends and interest) and pay no income tax on it. On the next $500 in income, the tax is 15 percent. After that, the child is taxed at your rate.

You can give a child up to $10,000 a year ($20,000 with your spouse) without paying any gift tax. So it is easy to shift income-producing assets to your child and save on taxes overall. If your rate is 28 percent, you would pay $280 in taxes on $1,000 in dividends or interest. Your child would pay only $75.00 (15 percent of $500). Savings: $205 a year.

After age fourteen, all unearned income after the first $500 but less than $17,850 is taxed at the child's rate, usually 15 percent.

▶ PUT KIDS ON THE PAYROLL

A child's *earned* income (distinct from unearned income; see previous two tips) is taxed at that child's tax rate. If you own a business, you can pay a child a salary for work performed, thus shifting some family income into a lower tax bracket. What's more, the child can take the full standard deduction against earned income, so a lot of the salary won't be taxed. There are other considerations, of course, and what you pay the child must bear some relationship to the value of the services performed.

▶ TRANSFER CAPITAL GAINS
TO YOUR KIDS

Suppose you want to sell a stock or a mutual fund you bought years ago, your basis price (what you bought it for) is $2,500, and it is now worth $12,500 (a very pleasant "suppose" indeed). If your tax rate is 28 percent, you'll pay $2,800 in taxes on your $10,000 gain. Since you and your spouse can give up to $20,000 a year to your child without paying a gift tax, you could instead make a gift of the stock to your child, who would pay only $1,500 in taxes on the sale.

One reason you might want to do this is because the stock represents money you had put away for college expenses anyway, so making the gift and having your child pay a tuition bill is a simple way of picking up an extra $1,300. Unfortunately, there's a catch-22 to transferring assets if your child will be applying for financial aid to attend college; see page 188.

▶ CONSIDER FILING SEPARATE TAX RETURNS

If you are a two-income family and either you or your spouse has high medical or business expenses, you may be able to reduce your tax bill by filing separate returns. If one of you had $3,750 in medical expenses and your joint adjusted gross income (AGI) was $50,000, for instance, you couldn't deduct any portion of your medical expenses because they are not more than 7.5 percent of AGI. If you filed separately, and your AGI was $25,000, you could deduct $1,875.

▶ BIG TAX REFUND EVERY YEAR? BIG MISTAKE

Some people seem to feel a tax refund check is a kind of gift from Uncle Sam. In fact, the gift has been from them to the IRS. By overwithholding taxes from your salary check, you are losing the interest income you could have earned on that money all year long.

If you usually get a refund check, review the number of deductions you have been claiming and consider adding to it.

Shopping Smart for Appliances, Furniture, Housewares, and Gifts

When they buy cars, most people are very aware of the miles-per-gallon numbers and realize that an 18-mile-a-gallon gas guzzler is going to cost a lot more over the long run than a car that gets 30 miles to the gallon. Yet as conscious as most people have become about the costs of energy, not many estimate the long-term costs before they buy a new appliance. In some areas of the country, the cost of the electricity to run a refrigerator during its working life will be five times the amount paid for it. Given a worst case energy scenario and a refrigerator that lasts for twenty years, even that cost could prove to be extremely conservative.

What this means is that the initial price of an appliance is only one factor—in many cases, the least important factor—in deciding how much that appliance will actually cost over its lifetime.

The same basic point (that initial cost is only one factor shoppers must evaluate) is also true when you make purchase decisions about furniture and housewares you hope to use for years to come. You will usually save money by paying more for quality goods and taking good care of them.

Having said that, there is still no reason to pay more than is necessary for those quality goods. Tips in this chapter suggest both strategies and specific sources for value-conscious shoppers.

▶ IS IT A STORE OR A BAZAAR?

The sign on the television set says: "Retail price $899.00. Our price $599.00." But the $599.00 is crossed out and "Special sale! $549.00" is written next to it. You are in a chain discount appliance store. What's your next step?

Quietly ask the sales clerk, out of hearing range of other customers, for the store's *best* price on the set. Often, without any further conversation, he'll call up the item on his computer terminal and come back with an even lower price than the supposed "special." At that point, you can either accept that price or make an even lower offer. Depending on all sorts of factors you can never know— including inventory levels, the chain's cash flow situation, and deals offered to the chain by that manufacturer—your offer might be accepted (although probably only after an act involving the clerk and a "manager") or rejected.

Many people are surprised by how many American retailers really do operate these days as open bazaars where quoted prices are only a starting point. But it is foolish not to attempt to negotiate a price on most high-ticket items. If you have decided on a specific brand and model, first call three or four stores to get their "best price." If one store's price is higher than another's, tell them so. You'll get a sense of how much maneuvering room there is on the price of that model.

Caution: The oldest trick of the bazaar operator is to quote you an extremely low price, whether by telephone or on the selling floor, then return from the stock room apologizing for being out of that model but ready to give you a terrific deal on an even better one. Tell the clerk you won't deal with a "bait-and-switch" operation and walk away. Slowly, of course. There just might be one left of the model you want after all.

▶ HAGGLE WITH OWNERS AND MANAGERS

In many stores, it is useless to ask clerks for discounts off ticketed prices. They aren't authorized to make special deals. But the owner or store manager definitely can. If you figure the store is working on a 40 percent markup and you ask for a 25 percent discount, an owner can quickly decide that a 15 percent profit is better than no sale at all. Remember to do your haggling quietly, out of hearing of other customers.

▶ SHOP AT THE END OF THE MONTH

Stores that have not met their monthly sales quotas may be more anxious to sell at reduced prices.

▶ SKIP EXTENDED WARRANTIES

See Chapter 3 for a discussion of the purpose of insurance, which is what an extended (beyond the time limit offered by the manufacturer) warranty on an appliance or an electronic product really is. In the case of the extended warranties offered (and usually aggressively sold) by retailers, the cost of the premium (the price of the warranty) is far higher than it should be, given the risk it protects you against.

The sales person you deal with probably gets a very healthy commission on sales of extended warranties. And the stores can afford the commissions, because many of them make as much or even more on the sale of the warranty as they do on the sale of the product itself.

A better idea: When you buy a new appliance, put half the money an extended warranty would have cost into a repair fund (see appendix). Unless you have bought an inferior product or are very unlucky, you should cover necessary repairs and save a lot of money.

▶ OFFER TO PAY CASH

If you offer to save stores the commission they pay when you use a credit card to make your purchases, they may be more willing to negotiate.

▶ ASK ABOUT CORPORATE DISCOUNTS

If you own your own company, many stores offer corporate discounts. For instance, if you are incorporated, Tiffany & Company will give you a 10 percent discount. Actually, if you have even a part-time business on the side, all you may need in some places is a business card, and perhaps a separate bank account.

▶ CHECK IT OUT FIRST IN *CONSUMER REPORTS*

Consumer Reports is published by the nonprofit Consumers Union, which independently tests different products and services and rates them in terms of safety, relative quality, and, sometimes, price competitiveness. This is the best single source of advice on buying just about anything from a VCR to a new convertible. The writing is straightforward, humorless, and for our tastes too often a bit self-righteous. We wouldn't buy a major appliance without knowing how *CR* rates different brands and models, but we skip its monthly report on readers' movie preferences and often disagree with taste panels that rate various foods and beverages. You may also sometimes be unable to find a model of a product highly rated by *CR*, because that model is no longer available.

If you are at a point in your life, perhaps just moving into a first house, where you are making a lot of major purchase decisions, a subscription to *Consumer Reports* could be an especially wise investment. Or do what we do: Make a few notes about some upcoming purchasing decisions, and drop in at your local library to check them out with *CR*.

▶ CALL AHEAD

When you are shopping for an unusual item or a specific model, telephone ahead to see if the store has it. A simple idea, but it can save a lot of time and cut down on travel expenses.

▶ USE THE ENERGYGUIDE LABELS ON APPLIANCES

Federal laws mandate the display of EnergyGuide labels on most home appliances. The efficiency ratings claimed on these labels are based on standardized tests and they are generally reliable.

The problem is, most people don't do much more than glance at the big dollar number in the middle of the label under the arrow. Let's say that on refrigerator Model A, the number is $80.00 (the annual cost of energy to run this model in an average home). On Model B, it is $110. You prefer Model B and decide that the extra $30.00 a year isn't too great a price to pay for the features you like.

You are making a hasty decision. Before you shop for any major appliance, make sure you check your latest utility bills to see how much *you* are paying per kilowatt hour for electricity. We, for instance, live in an area with particularly high energy costs. The $80.00 and $110 annual costs given on the two refrigerators in question are based on a national average cost of 8.04 cents per kilowatt hour. But our cost per kilowatt hour is 13.44 cents.

If you divide $80.00 by 8.04 cents, you know that Model A is expected to consume 952.38 kilowatt hours in an average home. Model B is expected to consume 1,309.52 kilowatt hours in that same average home. But our costs would be $128 annually for Model A (952.38 × 13.44 cents) and $176 (1,309.52 × 13.44 cents) for Model B. That makes the difference between the two models not $30.00, but $48.00 a year.

That annual difference of $48.00 adds up to $960 in twenty years, the life span of an average refrigerator. Actually, it would no doubt be much more, given inflation and our continuing grim prospects for energy bill increases. So we have a major incentive to buy the most energy-efficient refrigerator we can find, even if its initial cost is hundreds of dollars more.

Actually, of course, the initial cost of energy-efficient refrigerators is nearly always less, not more, than less efficient models, which are equipped with devices such as automatic ice makers and through-door dispensers.

▶ BUY A GAS RANGE WITH AN ELECTRONIC IGNITION SYSTEM

If you prefer cooking with gas, avoid ovens and ranges that use pilot lights. An automatic ignition system will cut down your gas use by at least one-third.

▶ CHECK UTILITY REBATES FOR EFFICIENT APPLIANCES

Many utilities now offer rebates to customers who buy energy-efficient air conditioners, refrigerators, freezers, heat pumps, water heaters, and other appliances. Before you buy a new major appliance, call the conservation office of your utility company and see what rebates are offered.

▶ BUY FROM MAIL-ORDER DISCOUNTERS

It's a lot easier to find deep discounts on appliances, furniture, and other items if you are looking for them and comparison shopping in a large metropolitan area, where strong competition holds prices down. If you live in a less-populated area, your best sources of bargains may be discount catalogs that you can order from by mail or telephone.

You can save on just about anything by mail, and often the prices are better than at any retail store in the country—large metropolitan area or not. If you are especially serious about finding the best mail-order bargains, hundreds of sources are described and rated within different categories by *The Wholesale-By-Mail Catalog*, a $14.95 paperback by The Print Project, published by HarperCollins.

The next few tips list mail-order sources for various kinds of merchandise that we, and our network of sources, have found particularly noteworthy for price, dependability, and service.

▶ AUDIO/APPLIANCES/VIDEO/ ELECTRONICS BY MAIL

None of these discount operations sell "gray-market" goods (products intended for sale in other countries; their manufacturers may not extend warranties on them for U.S. customers):

- *Dial-a-Brand,* 800-628-8260. In NY: 800-237-3220. TVs, VCRs, microwave ovens, air conditioners, large and small appliances. Prices quoted by phone.
- *Foto Electrical Supply Company,* 31 Essex St., New York, NY 10002. Price quotes by return mail (send SASE) on large appliances, cameras, TVs, audio and video equipment.
- *Wisconsin Discount Stereo,* 800-356-9514. In WI: 608-271-6889. Prices quoted by phone on audio and video equipment.
- *Crutchfield,* 800-336-5566, sells home and car audio equipment at good discounts. Prices quoted by phone.

▶ CAMERAS AND PHOTOGRAPHIC SUPPLIES BY MAIL

- *Porter's Camera Store,* Box 628, Cedar Falls, IA 50613. A free catalog any camera enthusiast should receive regularly, with a wide range of heavily discounted merchandise.
- *Mystic Color Lab,* 800-367-6061. A good film-processing service at terrific prices. Call for price quotes and free film mailers.

▶ FURNITURE BY MAIL

- *Quality Furniture Market of Lenoir,* 2034 Hickory Blvd. SW, Lenoir, NC 28645; 704-728-2946. Deeply discounted prices quoted by phone or mail on furniture and bedding from hundreds of different manufacturers.

- *Blackwelder's Industries,* 800-438-0201. In NC: 704-872-8922. Various catalogs available for nominal costs, refundable with purchase, on high-quality furniture, clocks, pianos, rugs, carpeting, and home accessories.
- *James Roy Furniture Company,* 15 E. 32nd St., New York, NY 10016; 212-679-2565. Prices quoted by phone or mail. Offers a minimum discount of one-third off suggested retail prices of furniture and bedding from hundreds of manufacturers.

▶ LIGHTING BY MAIL

- *Golden Valley Lighting,* 800-735-3377, sells table and floor lamps as well as lighting fixtures from most major manufacturers at discounts that range from 25 to 50 percent off retail prices. Make sure you have the exact model number and other necessary specifications when you call for a price quote. A catalog (price: $5.00) is also available.

▶ COOKWARE BY MAIL

- *A Cook's Wares,* 211 37th St., Beaver Falls, PA 15010; 412-846-9490. This mail order–only operation issues a catalog (price: $2.00) that features only the highest quality utensils, cookware, and foodstuffs at discounts of up to 50 percent.
- *Commercial Culinary,* P.O. Box 7258, Dept. NC-330, Arlington, VA 22207; 800-999-4949. Professional-quality cookware, cutlery, and appliances are available from this free catalog for up to 20 to 40 percent off retail.

▶ WALLPAPER BY MAIL

The companies listed below offer big discounts off the retail prices of virtually all wallpapers. Call with the name of the sample book and page number of the wallpaper you want to buy, and you will normally get an immediate price quote, usually 40 to 50 percent less than the suggested retail price and often 20 percent less than retail store discounters offer. Delivery is usually quick and efficient as well.

We have felt a bit guilty about using our local store's

sample books to choose wallpaper and then giving our
order to a lower-overhead competitor. So we were glad to
hear from Trudy Myers, a reader from Nanty-Glo, Pennsylvania. She wrote to tell us that when she quotes the
best price she gets from a mail-order supplier, her local
wallpaper store will match it. We'll try the same strategy
next time; as Ms. Myers points out, all the store can say
is no.

- *#1 Wallpaper,* 800-631-9341 or 800-423-0084
- *Bennington's,* 800-252-5060
- *Peerless,* 800-999-0898
- *Nationwide,* 800-488-9255

▶ CHINA, CRYSTAL, AND FLATWARE BY MAIL

- *Barrons* (800-538-6340; in MI: 313-344-4342) sells only
  by mail and will quote discounts of from 25 to 50 percent
  off the list prices of tableware and gifts. A catalog
  ($1.00) is also available.
- *The China Warehouse* (800-321-3212) will also quote
  discount prices off Waterford, Lenox, Royal Doulton,
  Towle, and other makers of china, crystal, and flatware.

Also: *Michael Fina* (800-BUY-FINA; in NY: 212-869-
8900); *Ross-Simon* (800-556-7376; in RI: 463-3100); *For-
tunoff's* (800-223-2326). These large retailers of jewelry,
gifts, and tableware all have good catalogs and may quote
prices by phone.

▶ CONSIDER SECONDS IN SHEETS AND TOWELS

Now that everyone knows about January white sales and
many, if not most, people wait for them, buying in January
no longer guarantees you the best bargains in sheets and
towels. In fact, manufacturers and department stores now
target January as a key sales month even for new merchandise. "On sale" and "marked down" don't necessarily mean
a thing.

The real bargains in sheets and towels are often found

in stores and factory outlets selling discontinued patterns and/or "seconds" of brand name merchandise. Most often, particularly with sheets and towels, it is very difficult to tell why a second is a second—a skipped stitch that won't affect wearability, or perhaps a slight variation in color that will be completely unnoticeable after one or two washings. Yet 50 to 75 percent discounts off list prices are common.

▶ SHEETS AND TOWELS BY MAIL

■ *Wamsutta/Springmaid Factory Outlets* (615-756-0805) is a chain of factory outlets operated by Spring Industries, which manufactures these two brands. If you aren't near a store, though, you can get a price quote by phone— up to 50 percent off retail, more for irregulars. Make sure you know the exact pattern, size, and color you want. If the number above (the outlet in Chattanooga, Tennessee) can't fill your order, ask for the number of another outlet that might have what you want. There is no central number to call to check stock in all of the outlets.

■ *Fieldcrest Cannon Factory Outlet Store* (for Fieldcrest products: 800-841-3336; for Cannon products: 800-237-3209) sells sheets, towels, blankets, bath rugs, and comforters at savings of 40 to 60 percent. Friends who can afford the best buy Fieldcrest Charisma sheets and towels this way, saving 60 percent on the most expensive mass-produced linens made in the United States. The telephone representatives are especially helpful.

▶ STOP BUYING GIFTS ON A DEADLINE

Most people make the same mistake over and over again, year after year, when they buy gifts. A week before Aunt Betty's birthday, and only then, they begin to think about what to get her. Then they rush out and buy something often not quite the right color or model. They also make a panicked whirlwind tour of stores two weeks before Christmas to buy for everyone on their list.

These are the kind of gift shoppers that swell retailer profits, but they are wasting their own time and money.

The alternative is simple and guaranteed effective. Except for unpredictable events like weddings, you know exactly who you will buy gifts for annually. Get a small, pocket-size notebook and make a list—every birthday and anniversary as well as everyone on your Christmas list. Update the list once a year to add graduations, bar mitzvahs, and other predictable special occasions.

Take this notebook with you whenever you think there is even a remote chance you will be shopping. Every time you enter a store of any kind, take ten seconds to review the list. Aunt Betty lives in Vermont and loves sweaters of all kinds. You are on vacation in Mexico in April and see two different sweaters in her size that would cost at least twice as much at home. Too bad her birthday was a month ago, right?

Wrong. Buy both. For the next two years, you won't have to spend frustrating hours shopping specifically for her. And you've bought two years' worth of birthday presents for the price of one.

Obviously, there are limits to your attic space. Ten years from now Aunt Betty might be two sizes larger. Styles may change. But the principle is an important one. The right gift, at the right price, simply doesn't appear as if by magic just because someone's birthday is a week away. The same sweater will nearly *always* cost much more on December 1 than it will in April. Different categories of merchandise are invariably cheaper during certain times of the year.

Remember to make notations of what you have bought in your notebook, or you are likely to forget what's up in the attic. Check items off as they are given. For safety's sake, because your notebook will become increasingly invaluable as a record of what you have given and what you've got stored, photocopy its pages from time to time and keep the copy in a safe place.

The only hard part of this is getting in the notebook habit. Once you have, you'll save hours of frustration and a lot of money—easily 30 percent or more.

▶ BEWARE THE $50.00 ROLEX

Of course you know you'll never find a real Rolex or

Cartier watch for the price of the illegal counterfeit you may encounter for sale at a flea market or on the street. Some people are tempted, though—it may look so "real." The sad fact is that, when compared directly with the original, the counterfeit invariably looks shoddy. Save yourself the embarrassment of being discovered.

▶ SHOP FACTORY OUTLETS

If you are unfamiliar with the factory outlet phenomenon, read the tips in Chapter 7 about shopping for clothing in factory outlets.

There are many factory outlets that sell merchandise other than clothing, of course. Among the many companies that sell seconds and irregulars, first-quality goods or both through factory outlets are Corning Revere (Corningware, Pyrex, Corelle, and Revereware brand cookware and dinnerware), Dansk (Scandinavian design cookware, flatware, gifts), Emerson Radio (Emerson and Scott electronic equipment), Hamilton Watches, Lenox (china), Oneida Silver (stainless and silverplated flatware), Royal Doulton (china), Samsonite (luggage), and Wamsutta/Springmaid (sheets, towels, linens).

Factory outlets are unquestionably sources of great bargains, but see Chapter 7 for shopping strategies to use.

▶ SHOPPING ABROAD: AVOIDING THE VAT

Most European countries, Japan, Israel, and Canada add a hidden tax (usually called a Value Added Tax) onto the cost of merchandise sold domestically. To encourage tourism, however, most also allow foreigners to escape some or all of this tax (which can be as high as 35 percent of the displayed retail purchase price), especially on expensive items.

In some stores, such as Harrods in London, the clerks are so accustomed to selling to foreigners that all you have to do is tell them you are an American and they'll make sure all of your tax-avoiding paperwork is done. You may have to work a bit harder elsewhere.

It doesn't make sense to ask about the VAT on low-cost items, and most countries spare their merchants the bother by setting a minimum purchase amount for a VAT refund (ranging from less than $100 in England to about $500 in Italy). Most countries also limit VAT refunds to purchases of merchandise, not to services.

Here's what to do:

- Before you buy a high-ticket item, ask if the store participates in the local VAT-reduction program, if your purchase qualifies, and how much your VAT refund will come to. Usually, the minimum amount necessary for a refund is not on a per-item basis but on a per-store basis—all purchases listed on one form. This makes shopping in as few places as possible preferable.
- Buy with a credit card if at all possible (it isn't everywhere) to get the best exchange rate on both the purchase and the refund.
- When you leave the country, you show the customs official all the VAT refund forms you have received from stores. You then either get a refund from customs then and there, or you mail validated forms back to the appropriate stores. They will either credit your account (if you paid by credit card) or eventually send you a refund check.
- Many countries permit stores to deduct the VAT from the purchase price if you don't take possession of the item but instead have it mailed to your home address. If such shipments are limited each day to merchandise worth less than $50.00, you don't have to pay a customs duty tax on them. Otherwise, you will have to pay U.S. duty and clearance expenses.

There can be enough of a hassle involved in all of this to discourage even a dedicated penny pincher if only a few dollars are involved, but it is more than worthwhile if you buy an expensive piece of jewelry or an antique vase.

▶ FURNISH A ROOM, APARTMENT, OR HOUSE ON THE CHEAP: IKEA

Out-and-out raves for an individual service, store, or product are rare in this book. If you have ever been inside an IKEA store, perhaps you will understand why we feel that this unique worldwide chain of warehouse-size home furnishing stores deserves special mention for people who are on a budget but care about style and at least a minimal level of quality.

There were only eight IKEAs in the United States as this book was going to press, six in the Northeast (in northern New Jersey, Long Island, and the Philadelphia, Washington, D.C., Baltimore, and Pittsburgh areas) and only two (in Fontana and Burbank, California) west of the Mississippi. But because they plan to open stores in the United States throughout the 1990s, at least half of our readers may soon be within driving distance of an IKEA.

It's worth a special trip if you have any interest in buying well-designed Scandinavian furniture, cabinets, china, linens, carpets, and lighting at prices at least 20 percent and often 40 to 50 percent lower than items of comparable quality anywhere else we know about. What's more, you can drive away with everything you want. IKEA tries to keep all 12,000 items they sell in stock at each location.

We're not suggesting you'll find heirloom quality here. IKEA is not a place to look for a dining room table you'll pass on in fifty years to your granddaughter. But we have a friend who, from scratch, handsomely furnished a one-bedroom apartment at IKEA for less than $3,400, including upholstered sofa ($298), two arm chairs ($89.00 each), a 9-foot-wide, 8-foot-high wall unit ($498), coffee table ($98.00), dining room table and four chairs ($335), a bedroom combination (bed, headboard, corner unit, cabinet, chest of drawers, desk: $734), and all the other necessities right down to table lamps ($7.50 and $24.00) and a twenty-piece set of dishes, cups and saucers ($13.00).

IKEA furniture consists of components that are packed flat; you have to assemble the furniture yourself. They don't sell by mail order, but you can get a good idea of what's in the stores by sending $2.00 (check or money order) for their 196-page four-color catalog. *IKEA,* 1000 Center Drive, Elizabeth, NJ 07202.

▶ BUY 364 DAYS EARLY

Don't you feel foolish, standing in a long line at the hardware store on December 24, waiting to pay for Christmas tree lights you know will cost 50 percent less at the same place (with shorter lines) two days later?

Christmas tree lights and ornaments, Christmas cards, holiday gift wrapping—all go on sale after December 25 for at least 50 percent off nearly everywhere. Even if you overestimate next year's needs, sooner or later everything you buy will be used.

The price of chocolate goes down right after Easter. Look for sales in wine and liquor stores right after New Year's Eve. And why not send a dozen roses to your valentine on February 15 (typically at a discount of at least 75 percent off February 14 prices) with a note declaring your ardor 364 days *ahead* of time? Now *that's* romantic (but don't try it as a *substitute* for a gift the day before).

▶ SHOP CHARITY THRIFT SHOPS

Many churches, synagogues, hospitals, and charitable organizations operate thrift shops either year round or on an occasional basis. Unless you are an inveterate shopper, forget 98 percent of them. The ones you are interested in are located in the most affluent sections of your metropolitan area. What gets donated to them is sometimes anything but thrift shop junk. Especially if you are looking for crystal, china, cutlery, and high quality cookware, try a couple of these first.

▶ CHECK PRICES ELSEWHERE
BEFORE COMPUTER SHOPPING

If you join an online service such as Prodigy, you'll be bombarded with "special offers" for all kinds of merchandise. It's easy to shop and buy via computer, but be careful about buying on impulse, and don't take it for granted that the "low" prices quoted are the lowest possible. In our experience, they rarely are.

Buying on impulse is what keeps the home shopping networks featured on cable television in business. We have a friend who loves the necklace she bought this way and firmly believes it was a great bargain. Maybe so. But we still find it difficult to understand how anyone can spend time watching this kind of television programming on the off-chance that something they really want will be offered for sale.

▶ CHOOSE THE MAILING LISTS YOU WANT TO BE ON

Why settle for what *they* want to send *you*? When you shop for the first time in a store you like, don't leave until you've asked to be put on its mailing list. Most retailers now have a mail-order capability, and many send advance notice to special customers when they are having a sale.

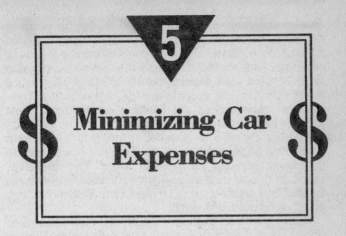

Minimizing Car Expenses

You should find some useful money-saving tips in this chapter no matter what kind of car you now own. But the first step in minimizing automobile expenses is to calculate what owning and operating a specific make and model will cost on an annual basis *before* you buy it.

One of the seldom-used keys to this process is estimating the price you will be able to get for a car when you sell it or trade it in. Some new cars will still be worth 50 percent of their purchase price four years later. Others will lose 75 percent of their value. If you buy a $16,000 car and trade it in for $8,000 four years later, it has cost you $2,000 a year plus fuel, maintenance, insurance, etc. If you buy a $14,000 car and trade it in for $3,500 four years later, your cost is $2,875 a year.

Nobody knows for sure how much any car will be worth years from now, of course, but one magazine—*Kiplinger's Personal Finance Magazine* (called *Changing Times* until July 1991), in its annual December issue—uses historical data on different manufacturers and models to estimate the resale value of the next model year's cars. It's good information to have. Whether you are buying a new or used car, you should also read the annual (April) auto issue of *Consumer Reports*, which is full of information about safety, repair records, prices, fuel economy, comfort and convenience, and handling on the road. Most libraries have both magazines on file.

Another expense to consider before you buy is what your insurance premiums will be. Similarly priced cars do not necessarily cost the same to insure. The difference, based on the car model's past and estimated future claims for theft and accidents, can be significant. Before you buy, talk to your insurance agent.

Working with an insurance agent, the magazines mentioned above, and prices negotiated with three different dealers in our area, we estimated annual costs on three similarly priced makes and models. The results are shown on page 85. The most expensive car in terms of initial price turned out to be well worth it.

When you next buy a car, use the same worksheet to establish estimated annual costs for each make and model you are considering. In fact, why not get your figures together now and estimate what your present car is costing you?

Once you actually analyze how much you spend to own and operate a car on an annual basis, you may come to some surprising conclusions. We have city friends who figure they saved at least $3,000 a year by getting rid of their car and renting one when they went away on weekends or on a vacation trip. Many people decide that the convenience of a second car is not worth the price.

▶ SAVE MORE THAN 50 PERCENT ON OIL CHANGES AND LUBRICATION

The fact is, today's cars need *less* normal maintenance than the gas guzzlers of the 1960s and 70s, and this kind of maintenance is easier to perform than it ever was. The complicated stuff in modern cars—electronics—usually gets replaced, not repaired. But you'd never know that

Annual Cost Worksheet for a New Car
(Sell/trade-in after 4 years and 60,000 miles)

	Car 1	Car 2	Car 3
A. Estimated purchase price (including taxes)	$17,100	$16,500	$17,400
B. Estimated resale value	6,000	4,800	7,830
C. Subtract B from A	11,100	11,700	9,570
D. Annual cost (C divided by 4 years)	2,775	2,925	2,393
E. Estimated annual insurance costs	1,200	1,150	920
F. Estimated cost of gas @ $1.20* a gallon, 15,000 miles a year (Divide 15,000 by estimated miles per gallon; multiply by $1.20)	857 (21 mpg)	720 (25 mpg)	643 (28 mpg)
G. Estimated average yearly maintenance	200	240	130
H. Estimated average yearly repairs/new parts	350	300	150
TOTAL ANNUAL COST	$ 5,382	$ 5,335	$ 4,236

*As this book was being prepared, the price of gas had fluctuated wildly within a six-month period. Adjust to current conditions.

when you look at the bloated bills most new car dealers hand you after a normal periodic warranty checkup.

If something is wrong or you even suspect something might be wrong with your car, by all means take it to a good mechanic or back to the dealer. Otherwise, use one of the franchised quick-lube-and-oil-change outlets. Their employees are trained to check all the essentials—belts, tires, brakes, etc.—lubricate what's necessary, and change the oil and oil filter.

Most manufacturers insist you must use factory-authorized parts to keep your warranty in force. No problem. Stop by the dealer's service center, buy a factory-authorized oil filter, and give it to the quick-lube outlet when you drive in. They will deduct the price of an oil filter from a bill that is nearly always at least 50 percent less than the same service would have cost at a car dealer or a full-service garage.

▶ DON'T PAY FOR WORTHLESS HIGHER OCTANE-RATED GAS

It is a waste of money ever to buy gasoline with a higher octane rating than is specified in your owner's manual (for most cars other than high-performance V-6s and V-8s, unleaded 87 octane). Some people think their car's engine needs a "super" gas treat now and then, that higher octane is somehow better for the engine. It isn't, despite the claims of the oil company ads.

One note of caution: Modern engines do need high-detergent fuels with special additives. Stations selling no-name brands may offer cheaper gas with the octane rating you require, but poor quality fuel can reduce efficiency and cause engine problems. Best to stick with the brands from the major oil companies.

▶ PAY CASH AND PUMP IT YOURSELF

Why pay cents a gallon extra to use a credit card when many stations offer a discount for cash sales? And why pay cents extra to have someone else pump gas for you, unless you are also getting some other useful service free? It's usually quicker, and requires hardly any more effort on your part, to use the self-service lane.

▶ BUY GAS EARLY IN THE MORNING

Especially in the hot summer months, you'll get more for your money—as much as 5 percent more—if you buy gas before the sun's heat has expanded the gas in the service station's fuel tank.

▶ DON'T TOP OFF YOUR FUEL TANK

Again, especially in hot weather, don't pump those few extra cents' worth in your tank after the automatic cut-off for a full tank. Heat will make the gas expand and overflow.

▶ USE YOUR CAR'S AIR CONDITIONER

In the past ten years, most new cars have become highly efficient in terms of aerodynamic design. Especially at higher speeds over long distances, you will waste more fuel in hot weather by opening windows and creating drag than you will by turning on the air conditioner.

▶ BABY PASSENGER? SAVE WITH A SAFETY SEAT LOANER

Some insurance companies and some communities have "loaner" programs that drastically cut the cost of a child safety seat. Check with your auto insurance agency, or send a stamped, self-addressed envelope along with a request for information on loaner programs in your area to the National Highway Traffic Safety Administration, Washington, D.C. 20590.

▶ CHECK TIRE PRESSURES REGULARLY

With the days of full-service-with-a-smile long gone at gas stations, most people put off checking tire pressures for months at a time. Yet you will lose about 2 percent fuel economy for every pound of pressure under the recommended pounds per square inch. Buy your own gauge (less than $5.00) and check tire pressures according to the manufacturer's recommendations at least once a month. You'll also save by prolonging the life of your tires.

Also check your wheel alignment whenever the car gets routine service. Even if wheels are only slightly out of line, they can affect gas mileage as well as shorten the life of tires.

▶ REMOVE YOUR ROOF RACK

If you're not using it regularly, take it off to reduce both drag and the car's total weight. Clean out the trunk, too. Extra weight reduces gas mileage.

▶ CHECK YOUR AIR FILTER

A dirty filter will lower gas mileage.

▶ DON'T IDLE A COLD ENGINE

Letting a car idle for two or three minutes to warm up a cold engine was once a recommended procedure. That's no longer true. Modern cars need only a few seconds of idling time; any longer and you are just wasting gas. In fact, you *reduce* engine wear when you move the car immediately, holding the speedometer down to under thirty for a couple of miles, then increasing your speed as you see the engine temperature begin to rise.

▶ USE AN ENGINE HEATER

They are common in Alaska and Maine, but even in less frigid climates an engine block heater (cost: $30.00–$40.00) can pay for itself in gas savings. Because it cuts down on engine wear, it will also prolong the life of your car.

▶ WAIT TO USE HEATERS AND AIR CONDITIONERS

In cold weather, save gas by waiting until the engine begins to warm up before turning on the heater. In hot weather, save gas by waiting until after you start the car to turn on the air conditioner.

▶ AVOID AIR-CONDITIONER PROBLEMS

Turn your car's unit on for ten or fifteen minutes every couple of weeks. This helps maintain coolant pressure and will lessen the odds of a breakdown.

▶ CHANGE A FEW DRIVING HABITS

If you can break a couple of bad driving habits, you can add at least 10 percent to your car's fuel efficiency.

- Minimize braking. Anticipate speed changes. When you see a red light ahead, take your foot off the accelerator and coast to it.
- Accelerate smoothly. Unless you are trying to fight your way onto a crowded freeway, there's no reason to jam your foot down on the pedal. Once you have reached your desired speed, keep a steady pressure on the accelerator, just enough to maintain speed.
- 55 saves money. The average car will use 17 percent less fuel when driven at 55 mph rather than 65 mph.
- Turn off the engine. It takes less gas to restart the car than it takes to let it idle for more than a minute.

▶ BUY A VACUUM GAUGE

If you are really serious about changing driving habits to get better gas mileage, consider buying a vacuum gauge. You can get one installed for about $60.00, and it will tell you at a glance when you are wasting gas and when you are getting optimum fuel efficiency.

▶ REDUCE THE COSTS OF BRIDGE TOLLS

Most bridge and tunnel authorities offer discounts if tickets or tokens are purchased in certain quantities. No doubt you buy this way if you commute over the same bridge most days. But even if you use a bridge only once a month, it is still probably worth your while to take advantage of reduced fare discounts, especially if there is no time limit on when the tokens have to be used.

▶ TRADE IN YOUR CAR JUST ONE YEAR LATER

The quality of all makes of cars has improved dramatically in the past fifteen years. If you got in the habit of trading a car in every three or four years, stretch that to four or five—or even seven to ten.

After it is three or four years old, the annual cost of owning a car drops dramatically. You'll probably spend more on repairs and replacement parts, but the years of big depreciation (the amount by which the car's value decreases simply because of age) are over, and insurance costs are lower. If you take proper care of your car and it remains rust-free, there's no reason not to get well over 100,000 miles of dependable service from it.

▶ BEFORE BUYING ANY CAR, CALL 800-424-9393

This is the toll-free number of the National Highway Traffic Safety Administration's Auto Safety Hotline. Call it to check on any safety recalls of the make, model, and year of any used car you are considering. You can also get information about how any new car model stacks up in the government's car crash tests.

▶ MAXIMIZE GAS MILEAGE ON ANY CAR YOU BUY

All new car specification sheets tell you how many miles per gallon the car supposedly will deliver in both city and highway driving conditions. All make clear you'll get better mileage with a manual transmission than with an automatic. No matter what make, model, or type of transmission you buy, if you want to get the best possible gas mileage you should also know:

- A car with a sun roof, even when it is closed, will get slightly worse gas mileage than the same car without one. An open sun roof can cost you a mile or more per gallon.
- A light-colored car reflects the sun, keeping the car

cooler in hot weather. The less your air conditioner has
to work, the better your fuel efficiency.

- Cruise control is a worthwhile option. It will help you
get better mileage when you are driving on a relatively
uncrowded, flat highway.
- In most of today's cars, overdrive is standard equipment. If it isn't in the car you choose, buy it as an
option. At higher speeds, it can cut your gas consump-
tion by 20 percent. In a manual-shift car, a fifth gear is
essentially the overdrive gear.

▶ BEFORE BUYING, KNOW WHAT YOU WANT

Don't start negotiating for any car before you have narrowed your choices to two or three models. The best way
to do this is to first spend some time in your library with
Consumer Reports and other publications, then visit a few
dealers and test drive a few cars.

Buying a car can be a confusing process, and dealers
love a customer who will accept their explanations. Start
shopping after your research is done, not while you are
doing it.

▶ KNOW THE DEALER'S COST BEFOREHAND

Consumer Reports' annual auto issue provides "cost factor" information on nearly all new car models that can help
you estimate how much the dealer had to pay the manufacturer for each one. Once you know this, you'll know how
meaningful offers to "knock five hundred" off the sticker
price really are.

For about $10.00 a computer printout, either *Consumer
Reports Auto Price Service* (Box 8005, Novi, MI 48050) or
Nationwide Auto Brokers (800-521-7257), will tell you the
dealer's cost not only on the basic make and model you
are considering, but also on all of its options and option
packages. Automobile salespeople don't enjoy dealing with
customers armed with such printouts, but they can save
you a lot of money.

You will have to pay something above the dealer's price, of course, to allow him some profit. And if you want a car that is in very short supply, the dealer may be selling every car he can get his hands on for sticker prices. One rule of thumb, though, says you should be able to negotiate a deal at 3 to 6 percent above dealer's cost.

▶ CHECK THE "DAY'S SUPPLY" NUMBERS

Will the dealer be willing to negotiate a favorable deal for you on the make and model you want? You can get a very good idea beforehand of how strong your bargaining position will be by checking the "day's supply" statistics published once a month in *Automotive News,* available in many libraries and often published in the financial pages of some newspapers. If the number of cars sitting on dealers' lots is equivalent to a hundred days' supply at the current rate of sale, you are far more likely to get a terrific deal than if there is only a twenty days' supply. The higher the days' supply, the more likely the dealer will be under pressure to move cars.

▶ CHECK ON MANUFACTURER'S INCENTIVES

Automotive News has another useful feature, a weekly column called "Incentive Watch" that lists all the rebate and financing deals currently offered by domestic and foreign manufacturers. It provides details—the amount of the rebates and expiration dates—not only for consumer deals, but also for the incentives available to dealers to sell certain makes and models. Deduct the dealer's rebate from the car's invoice price to know the true current wholesale price of the car.

▶ WHILE NEGOTIATING, DON'T TELL THE DEALER HOW YOU'LL PAY

No matter how many times the salesperson asks (and ask they all will), don't talk about how you'll pay until you have reached a definite, final agreement on how much. If pressed, tell them you will pay cash. And if asked about a trade-in during the negotiating process, tell them you won't be trading in your old car. You can always change your mind after you have established the price of the new one.

Why the secrecy? You don't spend your life negotiating car deals; they do. It is in your interest to keep the discussion as simple as possible. Once financing and trade-ins become part of the picture, the deal will get so complicated you'll never know just how much your new car actually cost.

▶ PAY CASH IF YOU CAN

Sorry, but it's always a better penny-pinching strategy than any kind of loan. (See Chapter 8 about different kinds of loans.)

▶ ASK FOR MANUFACTURER'S REBATES UP FRONT

If the manufacturer is advertising rebates, tell the dealer you want the rebate deducted from the final negotiated price of the car, not in a check mailed later on from the manufacturer. You'll save on sales tax this way.

▶ FIRM BUT PLEASANT WORKS BEST

It's easy to forget a lot of good advice on how to buy a car once you are negotiating with a skillful salesperson. You'll be subjected to sales techniques and psychological tricks that have worked in millions of negotiations. If you've done your homework, though, you'll know a lot about how strong your bargaining position is. Smile, stay with it, and be prepared to walk away. There are always other dealers.

▶ JOIN AUTOVANTAGE ON-LINE

If you have access to a computer and a modem, *Autovantage* (800-843-7777; three-month free trial membership; $49.00 annual fee thereafter) offers a number of services and discounts. Among them:

- Prenegotiated discounts on most new cars. You call Autovantage with the make, model, and options you want. They tell you the dealer's invoice price and the amount you should add to that for dealer profit. They fax that information to a participating new car dealer near you, where you can then buy the car at that preestablished discounted price. No fuss, no bother. When we checked this service out, we found the price close to what we got when we negotiated on our own. If you are a bit shy or just hate negotiating with car salesmen, this is a useful service.
- New car summaries. Dealer costs, operating expenses, resale projections, standard equipment, and options on most makes of new cars. A good way to comparison-shop at home.
- Discounts (typically 10 percent) at places like AAMCO, Goodyear, K mart Auto Centers, Firestone, Meineke, etc.

▶ GET PRENEGOTIATED PRICES ON A NEW CAR

Autovantage (previous tip) isn't the only way to avoid the hassle of haggling with car salespeople. You might also want to look into *CarBargains* (800-475-7283; fee: $96.00), which is run by the Center for the Study of Services, a nonprofit consumer group in Washington, D.C. You tell CarBargains the make and model you want. They then get bids from at least five dealers in your area and submit all of these bids to you, along with complete information on dealer invoice costs. The fee is a bit stiff, but solid bids from five dealers are well worth having. Also, CarBargains will follow up if a dealer reneges on a bid.

Auto brokers—independent sales organizations that work for dealers, not for you—are another way to get discounted prices on a new car. You'll see their ads in classified sections of newspapers, and calls to a couple of them are an easy way to establish a price that you may or may not be able to get on your own. If you can't find an ad for an auto broker in your newspaper, try *Nationwide Auto Brokers* (800-521-7257).

▶ **CHECK LOAN RATES BEFORE YOU SHOP**

If you must borrow money to buy a car, talk to your bank (and check loan rates in other banks) before you negotiate with the dealer. Particularly in these days of dealers' either/or choices between rebates and low manufacturer financing, it is difficult to evaluate different deals. Are you better off taking a $1,000 rebate and financing with your bank? Or should you skip the rebate and pay the lower interest rate offered by the manufacturer? You'll have to work the numbers out yourself (or ask a friendly accountant to do it), but generally the more you have to borrow, the more likely it is that the low financing is a better choice. (See Chapter 8 for more on auto loans.)

▶ **AVOID DEALERS' LOANS**

A low interest rate offered as a special deal by the manufacturer is different from a normal dealer loan on an automobile. It is rarely a good idea to borrow from the dealer. See Chapter 8 for details.

▶ **NEVER SHOP FOR A MONTHLY PAYMENT AMOUNT**

The worst possible mistake you can make when negotiating with a car dealer is to tell him how much you can pay for a car on a monthly basis. If he knows that's your primary concern, he'll tailor a loan to fit that amount, adding more monthly payments, higher interest rates, and a far higher total price. *Always* negotiate for a car as if you are going to be a cash buyer.

▶ **SKIP THE DEALER'S RUSTPROOFING OPTION**

It is not only useless, it may actually be damaging. All new cars today are rustproofed at the factory and all manufacturers provide a long-term anti-corrosion warranty. The compounds and drilling involved in additional rustproofing can disturb what was done at the factory. Dealer rustproofing has survived for only one reason: It is highly profitable for dealers.

▶ SKIP THE DEALER'S EXTENDED WARRANTY

See Chapter 4 on extended warranties. Same scam. Instead, buy a car with a good frequency-of-repair history.

▶ IN FACT, SKIP ALL THE DEALER'S "EXTRAS"

You've negotiated a terrific deal, so good that you wonder how the dealer can afford to take so little profit. There are smiles and handshakes all around. Now the dealer is writing out the order.

Be careful. Rustproofing and extended warranties are only two of the extra services dealers can add on, and often these add-ons are the source of most of their profit. The easiest way to handle this is to remember that you have bought a car, period. Nothing else. Maybe there are exceptions to the rule at some dealers, but we've never encountered any: If you want a dealer extra, you can find it somewhere else better and cheaper.

Among the extras you may be offered, or even told you have to buy:

- *Fabric protection.* Buy your own can of Scotchgard.
- *Glaze protection.* An extra coat of wax. Buy it at a car wash for much less.
- *Any kind of insurance.* See Chapter 3, but you absolutely don't want to buy accident, health, disability, or credit life insurance from your dealer.
- *Preparation charges.* The factory price of the car includes dealer preparation charges. Don't pay any extra charges. Inspect the car when you receive it, and don't accept it if it isn't clean inside and out.
- *Processing fees.* There may even be a preprinted "processing fee" of $50.00 or $100 in the dealer's sales

agreement. Processing what? This is simply a way for the dealer to get back $50.00 or $100 of the money you have saved by hanging tough in your negotiations about price. Hang tough again. Cross it out. If the dealer objects, tell him you're willing to buy the car elsewhere rather than get taken by as obvious a scam as this. By now he should be taking you very seriously.

▶ LEASING IS NOT FOR PENNY PINCHERS

Like any other rule, there are probably exceptions to this one. And leasing may make some economic sense if you buy a car through a business you own. But when you compare the true annual costs of each, you are normally better off buying a car rather than leasing it.

The reason leasing has become so popular is that it is a way to drive a car without much of a down payment and with lower monthly payments. It is especially seductive if you want a luxury car that costs more than $30,000. But you will have borrowed the car; you won't own it. At the end of four years, or whatever the term of the lease, you will have nothing to show for your payments. Because you won't have a hard asset, a car worth X dollars, your true annual cost will invariably be higher than if you had bought the car four years earlier.

▶ BEFORE BUYING A USED CAR, CALL 900-258-2886

At $1.50 a minute, charged to your phone bill, this call to *Consumer Reports Used Car Price Source* is a bargain. You will get the up-to-the-minute market value for any used car up to seven years old—adjusted for mileage, condition, the major options (air conditioning, automatic transmission, etc.) on the car you are considering, and in your geographic area.

If you ask, you can also find out how *Consumer Reports* rates the model in terms of its frequency-of-repair record (also available in the April issue of the magazine, which you can find at nearly any public library).

► USE THE NADA BLUE BOOK

Every month, the National Automobile Dealers Association (NADA) publishes its *Official Used Car Guide* in eight regional editions. Available at most libraries, the NADA guide is generally referred to as "the blue book," although it isn't blue. While we think the *Consumer Reports* used-car valuation (previous tip) is worth the extra money, you should also know what the current blue book says about any used car you are seriously considering.

The most important information in the blue book is the current average trade-in price of the car when it is in good condition. You will also find "average retail" prices, "average loan" values (what a bank would lend you on the car), current values of various optional equipment, and mileage tables that tell you whether to add or subtract from the average price.

Your goal when negotiating price is to pay as little as possible over the NADA trade-in price—certainly nothing like the "retail" price also listed in the guide. How much more? That depends on the usual supply-and-demand factors as well as on whom you are buying it from; you might get a better deal from an owner selling direct than from a dealer.

► BUT BEWARE THE DEALER'S BLUE BOOK

It may be a fake, published especially for dealers. Some—not all—dealers will pull out one of these (listing higher prices than in the authentic books) when a potential used car customer insists on knowing blue-book prices.

New car buyers may also encounter fake blue books when negotiating trade-in prices on their old cars. Check your library's NADA guide price before you talk to anyone about trading it in.

► SELL YOUR OLD CAR YOURSELF

Although you will nearly always get more by selling your old car yourself rather than trading it in, think twice before doing it, because it can be a frustrating experience. It may also take longer (adding to insurance and upkeep costs) and require more advertising (more extra costs) than you initially plan on. Especially if you live in a high sales-tax area, factor that into your decision. If you buy a new car for $15,000, sales tax at 8 percent is $1,200. If, as part of that deal, you trade in a car for $5,000, your sales tax is reduced by $400 (you pay only 8 percent of the $10,000 difference). That means you will have to get $5,400 for the car elsewhere to match the dealer's $5,000 offer.

▶ BUT ESTABLISH THE TRUE TRADE-IN PRICE BEFOREHAND

Whatever *Consumer Reports* and the NADA blue book tell you about prices, car salespeople will give you a dozen reasons why they don't pertain to your car. The acid test comes when you actually try to sell it.

It will take a couple of hours, but shop the car around to at least three dealers in your area who buy used cars. Simply tell them you are definitely selling the car, you are getting prices at four or five different places, and you will be back the same day to sell it to whoever gives you the best price.

The highest price you get is what you should tell your new car salesperson you'll accept as a trade-in price. In fact, tell him who gave you that price. Chances are, he'll factor in the sales-tax differential (see previous tip), but make sure he doesn't also use this as an opportunity to go back and renegotiate the deal you've already made on the new car.

▶ BUY A NOT-QUITE-NEW CAR

There are fewer "nearly new" low-mileage cars on dealers' lots now than there were back in 1990, mainly because too many people became aware of the bargains that resulted from manufacturer "buyback" arrangements with car-rental companies. In some cases, cars only three months old—many with fewer than 10,000 miles on their odometers—were bought back and then auctioned to dealers who resold them for 20 to 30 percent less than similarly equipped new models.

Recently, after hearing cries of outrage from new car dealers who had to compete with "nearly new" sales, manufacturers have generally extended buyback agreements to five or six months. Even with a few more miles on them, though, these cars (and other highly desirable "nearly news" generally traded in by people in the automotive industry) can still be very attractive buys. The warranty coverage is usually transferable (don't buy unless it is), although there may be a small fee involved.

As with most "terrific deals," especially those involving the automobile industry, you've got to be careful before you sign a sales agreement. Here are a few absolute rules to follow:

- Know the price of a comparably equipped new model of the car. Go to another dealer and negotiate a price on one. If the nearly new doesn't save you at least 20 percent, think long and hard before buying it. The dealer probably got it for at least a 30 percent discount off the retail price of the new model.
- Don't even consider buying a nearly new unless the dealer will show you the title to the car before you sign a purchase agreement. The title will tell you who owned it last. Was it Kamikaze Auto Rental or a vice-president of an auto company? The latter's car is probably a better buy. The title will also give you the odometer reading at the time of ownership transferal. Make sure what's on the car's odometer agrees.
- The dealer should be able to show you a mandatory written inspection record done on the car right after it was bought at auction. If an inspection wasn't done within two weeks after the auction, the manufacturer might not honor the warranty if something goes wrong.
- Finally, spend the money to have an independent mechanic/garage test drive the car, check it out for any problems, and see if there is any reason to be suspicious about the odometer reading.

▶ BUY A NOT-YET-OLD CAR

"Not-yet-old" is a term coined by a friend who, every three years, buys a luxury car that is two or three years old. Depending on the make and model, most cars depreciate in value from 30 to 45 percent in their first two years. After that, depreciation slows down considerably.

Our friend says he pays extra for a very clean, obviously well-cared-for car, and always has a mechanic inspect it first. When he sells the car three years later (when it is five or six years old) he gets about 60 percent of what he originally paid for it. He figures his annual costs of driving a Mercedes for the past twenty years have been about the same as if he had traded in a new Ford every two or three years.

This is a valid strategy, but it works best if you buy used luxury cars with superior frequency-of-repair records.

▶ CAR POOL

If your drive to and from work each day adds up to fifteen miles, you'll put over 3,500 miles a year on your car. Just cutting that in half—by finding one person to car-pool with—will save you hundreds of dollars. If your car pool allows you to use a special rush-hour lane reserved for buses and cars with more than a certain number of people in them, you'll also save time.

Many companies have van pools. Look into joining one of them.

▶ USE PUBLIC TRANSPORTATION

Taking a bus or train is invariably cheaper than driving your own car, and by not subjecting your car to everyday bumper-to-bumper traffic jams to and from work, you'll extend its life by years.

▶ BUY A BICYCLE

Other than walking, there's no better, healthier way to minimize transportation expenses. Count up all those two-mile trips by car to the 7-Eleven and consider how much you could save in a year by substituting a bike equipped with a basket.

Because this book is about penny pinching, we don't always mention environmental benefits of certain strategies. But we do care about them. Car pooling and riding buses, trains, and bicycles, like many other penny-pinching ideas, are earth-friendly activities.

6

Cutting the Costs of Vacations, Travel, and Dining Out

Like fresh fish and bagels, the products of the travel industry are perishable—but even more so. There may be some way for a bagel maker to sell his stale product for a reduced price a day later, but there is no way to sell either an empty seat after the airliner takes off or a vacant hotel room the morning after.

Car rental companies, airlines, hotels, resorts, and cruise ships all have high fixed overhead costs. Their expensive buildings, cars, airplanes, and ships—along with the people it takes to operate them—must be paid for whether 50 percent or 100 percent of the rooms and seats are occupied. To make a profit, the number of unoccupied rooms and seats must be held to a minimum, even if that means reducing prices drastically.

The result is a bewildering system of ever-changing fare structures, hidden discounts, concealed wholesaler rates, and promotional deals. The travel industry periodically makes an effort to reform the system. In 1992, all of the major U.S. airlines, led by American, announced with great fanfare a restructuring of fares. Essentially, fare structures were simplified and discounts standardized for those who made 7- or 21-day advance purchases of coach tickets.

This restructuring was supposed to eliminate secret corporate discounts and other abuses. Will it end the too-common experience of someone paying a $500 airline fare who discovers on the plane that the person in the next seat paid $99.00? We wouldn't bet on it. Competition is simply too fierce, and the pressure to fill empty seats is not going to change. There are always going to be penny-pinching deals in air travel for those willing to look for them.

The tips in this chapter will help you cut through the confusion to get the best deals possible for your travel dollar. A few of them cover similar ground: If you join a last-minute travel club, for instance, you may get benefits that make a half-price coupon directory superfluous. Some of them make sense only if you travel a lot: If you would use only one or two coupons from a half-price coupon directory, don't buy one.

If you are young (usually 26 or younger, especially if you are a student) or old (50 or over, or even better, 62 or over), you have opportunities for discount travel denied those in the age groups in between. The travel industry is keenly aware that people over 50 are responsible for more than 80 percent of the total dollars spent on nonbusiness travel. Also, students and retired people are often flexible about scheduling, so they can fill airplane seats and hotel rooms that would otherwise remain vacant during nonpeak times. At the end of this chapter, there are some specific tips for these two groups.

Whichever tips you decide are right for you, here are three guidelines that are always operative:

- Comparison shopping is essential.
- Discounts are the norm, not the exception, throughout

the travel industry. Look for them. Ask for them. Bashfulness is not a virtue among penny pinchers.

■ Establishing a relationship with a savvy travel agent who is willing to work hard to save you money can be an enormous time saver. The best way to do this is to make sure your agent gets commissions on your easy reservations as well as your more difficult ones. And the more work you can do yourself before you put your agent to work, the better your relationship will be. Clients who habitually change their minds and cancel reservations will not get first-rate service.

▶ OUT OF *WHOSE* SEASON?

The luxury Caribbean resort that charges $500 a day in March may reduce that price by as much as 50 percent six weeks later. By May, airlines flying to the Caribbean usually drop rates as well. Not much else has changed. The temperature may be 2 or 3 degrees hotter, but the prevailing island breezes make that difference barely perceptible. The tennis courts and golf course will be less crowded, and the duty-free stores often mark things down off-season.

You can also get terrific off-season bargains in most ski resorts. No snow, but you might not mind when you consider you can get summer mountain scenery, golf, tennis, lake swimming, hotel rooms, condo rentals, and restaurant meals at huge discounts from peak winter rates.

Is it really worth a 40 or 50 percent premium to go in season? Your answer may well be yes, if the choice is the Maine coast in January or July. But many choices aren't that dramatic. And sophisticated travelers, even those who aren't purposely penny pinching, avoid places like Paris in August, when the Parisians flee from their city and busloads of tourists take it over.

▶ BECOME YOUR OWN TRAVEL AGENT

It is nearly impossible these days to find a travel agent willing to investigate all the "what-if" scenarios about airline travel a penny pincher may have. Shopping by telephone among individual airlines is even more hopeless. But if you have a home computer and a modem, or have access to one, there's an inexpensive solution.

Until 1989, the only way a home computer user could access an airline reservation system was to pay by the minute, a very expensive process if you were trying to figure out a complicated schedule or search for the lowest fares. That was before the introduction of Prodigy (currently $12.95 a month plus local telephone usage fees; call 800-284-5933 for information). Obviously, you must either travel often or find the many other services offered by Prodigy worthwhile to justify the monthly expense. But its flat monthly fee gives you unlimited access to Eaasy Sabre, American Airlines' reservation program.

If you like, using Eaasy Sabre, you can actually book reservations, charge your ticket to your credit card, and receive tickets by mail. But we prefer simply to shop by computer, pinning down the exact flight and fare we want (although American Airlines flights seem to turn up first on many lists of what's available, you'll get full information on all airlines). Then we call a good travel agent to make those reservations. The travel agent is paid by the airline, not you, and in appreciation for getting such an easy commission should be willing to spend some extra time helping you with the rest of your itinerary.

▶ BUY AIRLINE TICKETS FROM A CONSOLIDATOR

When airlines can't sell all the seats on a flight, despite their own promotions and special discounts, they may sell them to a ticket broker—a "consolidator"—at a wholesale price. The consolidator is then able to offer tickets for anywhere from 15 to 50 percent below normal prices. Consolidators sell to travel agents (some sell only to travel agents) as well as direct to the public, often through newspaper ads. Unless you ask your travel agent to check on the availability of a consolidator ticket, that option will usually not be explored.

Most consolidators specialize in international flights, but some also sell tickets for heavily traveled domestic routes. It's all perfectly legal, and quite safe to deal directly if it's a well-established, reputable company. Tickets are nearly always sold on a nonrefundable basis.

Although the companies listed below will hold your payment in escrow until your flight departs (not all consolidators will), it's a good idea to pay with a credit card so you can cancel easily if something goes wrong. Also, get your tickets as soon as possible after ordering so that you'll have time to correct any mistakes.

The down side: You may not fly at the most convenient time or by the most direct route. You may be told you can't get an advance seat assignment. You can't switch airlines at the last minute. You may not get frequent flier credit for the miles flown. And sometimes airlines offer promotional fares that are as good or even better than what a consolidator can offer. In many such cases, however, that promotional fare may be loaded down with restrictions (travel only between Tuesday and Thursday and stay over one Saturday if the moon is full) that you can't live with.

Some consolidators, including those below marked with an asterisk, also offer discounts on hotels.

As usual, the number one rule for an airline traveler who wants to save money is to shop all the alternatives before buying.

A few consolidators to call for more information: *Travac* (800-872-8800; NY 212-563-3303); *UniTravel** (800-325-2222; MO 314-569-0900); *Access International** (800-825-3633; NY 212-465-0707); *Jetway** (800-421-8771; CA 213-382-2477).

▶ TRAVEL FIRST CLASS (MAYBE)

If you belong to the frequent flier program of most major airlines (including American, Delta, and United), you probably know you can trade in some of your accumulated mileage to upgrade a coach ticket to first class. Less well known is that members can often purchase an upgrade at the airport for very little money, typically $25.00 or $30.00

for a 1,000-mile flight. Unfortunately, you can only get the upgrade when you have bought a full-price coach ticket. It's best to arrive early to get your request in, since most upgrades (although not all) are sold on a standby basis.

▶ ASK YOUR TRAVEL AGENT ABOUT FARE ASSURANCE

Some travel agents now have access to a fare assurance program that automatically checks airline computers on a daily basis *after* you buy your ticket, to see if you qualify for any newly available lower fares until twenty-four hours before your flight.

▶ CHECK ON NESTED FARES

The bizarre structure of airline fares sometimes makes it advantageous to throw tickets away. A regularly priced round-trip coach ticket that called for you to leave City A on Tuesday and return from City B on Thursday might cost $800. But *two* round-trip discount fares between the same two cities that called for a minimum stay of seven days, including one Saturday night, might cost only $200 each. You would save $400 by throwing away one of the tickets from each round trip. Especially if you are flying midweek, ask your travel agent to look into this alternative.

▶ FLY VIA A "HIDDEN" CITY

When it comes to airline tickets, comparison shopping isn't always simply a matter of finding the lowest-priced ticket from City A to City B. It is entirely possible that if you buy a ticket for a flight that goes from City A to City C but stops at City B on the way, it will be cheaper than a ticket for the flight from City A to City B. You simply get off at City B and throw the rest of your ticket away.

If you do find a deal like this, make sure your luggage can be carried on the plane. Don't book on a round-trip basis, because you would be a "no-show" on the return flight from City C. And do things quietly; the airlines don't like this practice at all. In a few cases, they have actually billed travel agencies for the difference in fares.

▶ FLY VIA AN INTERMEDIATE CITY

Very often, a ticket for a direct flight between City A and City C is more expensive than two tickets, one that takes you from City A to City B, the other going from City B to City C. You may have to travel quite a few extra miles (in some cases, you may even have to go in the opposite direction of your eventual destination) and it will take some extra time. You may even fly two different airlines. But savings can be considerable.

How can you know when such a deal is possible? All the major airlines utilize "hub" airports. If you know that a cheap flight from City A to that hub is available, also check out flights from the hub to your destination. Major hubs include Atlanta (Delta), Chicago (United, American), Dallas (American), Northwest (Minneapolis), St. Louis (TWA), Pittsburgh (USAir), and Newark (Continental), but all major airlines have a few hubs each.

▶ USE A FREQUENT FLIER CREDIT CARD

See Chapter 8, page 159.

▶ JOIN "AIR MILES" TRAVEL REWARDS

This program, new in the United States and Canada but well established in the United Kingdom, was introduced shortly before the manuscript deadline for this edition. We haven't had time to evaluate it, but you may want to try it anyway. There's no enrollment fee, so why not?

The "Air Miles" program rewards purchasers of participating brand products and services with a certain number of free miles on American Airlines, United, USAir, or Air Canada. Examples given in the program brochure included 100 miles for a one-year subscription to *Time* magazine, 100 miles for a pair of glasses from the LensCrafter chain, and 4 miles for a gallon of Pine Sol cleaner. These aren't frequent flier "points"; each mile rewarded is for one mile of free travel on a round-trip ticket. So you would need

812 miles for a round-trip coach ticket between Boston and Washington. You can't mix Air Miles credits with other frequent flier program credits.

Among the sponsor companies announced are General Cinema Theaters, Hyatt Hotels, Frito-Lay, Hertz, and Prodigy.

It is an interesting idea. We don't yet know, for example, if buying nine gift subscriptions to *Time* would entitle us to a free round-trip ticket between Boston and Washington. We wonder, too, whether we want to go through the hassle of clipping and mailing the UPC code from a gallon of Pine Sol to get credited with four miles. If Air Miles signs up enough sponsoring companies whose products or services you would use anyway, however, the hassle could be worthwhile. To enroll, call 800-222-2247.

▶ EXCESS BAGGAGE? SEND IT AHEAD

If you are moving a season's wardrobe or a lot of household items, it can be cheaper—and certainly far more convenient—to send them ahead via UPS than to pay extra baggage charges to an airline.

▶ USE CORPORATE DISCOUNT RATES FOR PERSONAL TRAVEL

If corporate discounts are available when you are traveling for your company, there is usually no reason why you can't ask for them when traveling for personal reasons.

▶ CALL FOR A CONDO

One easy way to save on a family vacation is to rent a condominium instead of paying for hotel rooms. A washer, dryer, and kitchen facilities can help cut costs dramatically. You can check out availabilities and prices of condos in any U.S. vacation area by calling *Condo Network* at 800-874-1411. This is particularly handy when time is short. If you have the time, you'll get a wider selection by also writing local rental agents in the area. You'll see their ads in the classified sections of travel magazines.

► ENROLL THE WHOLE FAMILY IN FREQUENT FLIER PROGRAMS

It is foolish not to join an airline's frequent flier program, even if you don't think you'll use the airline again. In an age of airline mergers and rapidly changing personal plans, who knows? It takes no effort at all to join most of the programs right at the airport. Maintain a file of what you've earned in each of the programs, and it may very well affect your choice of airline sometime in the future.

Even if your children don't fly often, enroll them, too. Over a few years' time, they may well qualify for free trips.

► USE FREQUENT FLIER MILEAGE WISELY

The temptation is to use frequent flier mileage for a free ticket as soon as you have enough saved up. That's not always the best strategy.

Always check first to see what special deals are possible. If the airlines are engaged in one of their periodic promotional price wars, you might be better off buying a ticket, collecting more frequent flier mileage on that cheaper-than-usual flight, and using the mileage later when prices are back to normal.

► TURN OFF THE HOT WATER HEATER WHILE YOU'RE AWAY

Most people remember to turn the thermostat down when they're going to be away from an empty house for any length of time. But why pay to keep hot water available if nobody is there to use it? If you're going to be away long enough, also clean out the refrigerator and freezer and turn them off. When you do, leave the doors open a bit to prevent mold, and leave an open box of baking soda inside.

► CARRY A 100-WATT LIGHT BULB

Even luxury hotels often discourage inveterate readers by putting 40-watt bulbs in night table lamps, and few hotel housekeepers in our experience have been able to supply brighter substitutes. After a midnight search a few years ago that finally resulted in the purchase of the world's most expensive single bulb, we've packed our own whenever we are headed for a hotel. We also bring along an extension cord.

▶ CONSIDER BUDGET MOTELS

Our idea of penny pinching is not to sacrifice comfort or convenience for money. But when we are traveling by car in the United States and want only a clean, quiet, comfortable room for the night—knowing we will leave early the next morning and won't want room service, a swim in the pool, or help with our baggage—we choose one of the budget chains (*Hampton Inn, Super 8, Budgetel, Red Roof*). The beds, bathrooms, and TVs are just as good as they are in higher priced motels. For $40.00 or less a night, we've never been disappointed.

▶ BOOK HOTEL ROOMS AT THE LAST MINUTE

It's risky if there's a big convention in town or it is "in season" for a particular city. But normally—and especially if there are stories in newspaper financial pages about low occupancy rates—you can negotiate a good rate when you call a few hotels on your arrival date. Simply ask for the lowest rate for the type of accommodations you want, and tell them you'll call back to confirm if you like what is offered.

This is a particularly effective strategy with smaller hotels. Before you leave, narrow your choices by checking guide books (*Frommer's, Fodor's,* etc.) that list and rate them.

▶ SPEND WEEKEND VACATIONS IN BIG CITIES

Deluxe and first class hotels in major cities are highly dependent on business travelers, who tend to arrive on Monday morning and leave on Friday. That means a lot of expensive hotel rooms are difficult to fill on Friday, Saturday, and Sunday nights. Nearly all but the upper tier of big city luxury hotels now offer some kind of promotional packages that can cut room rates by more than 50 percent and often include free breakfasts and other extras. Call the 800 line of any of the nationwide chains (*Hilton, Hyatt, Marriott, Ritz-Carlton, Westin,* etc.) for information about a city you are interested in, as well as chain-wide promotions. The travel section of your newspaper and the travel magazines (*Travel and Leisure, Travel, Sunset,* etc.) will also feature ads about special weekend packages.

Except in resort areas and New York City, the same phenomenon makes car rentals from a big city location a lot cheaper over the weekend.

▶ GO BACK TO COLLEGE

Because we could never seem to visit each other at home, we arranged to meet old friends for a weekend in the university town where two of us had gone to college, easy driving distance for both couples. By the time we left, we realized we had stumbled onto an incredible short vacation bargain—one that can be duplicated in dozens of other university towns, regardless of whether you are an alumnus.

There was no alumni reunion going on (when prices for rooms more than double), but for less than a third of the cost in a major city we saw an exciting Division I basketball game, visited a small but first class art museum, attended a concert given by a world-renowned pianist, and had dinner at two first-rate restaurants.

University towns all seem to have a lot of restaurant bargains, modestly priced accommodations, and a surprising variety of major cultural and sporting events. Our total bill for the weekend—two nights, motel room, six meals (two with wine), all tickets—was $212, about the cost of a New York City hotel room on a Tuesday night.

▶ GO ON THE SPUR OF THE MOMENT

Not everyone can afford to drop everything and fly off for a vacation on forty-eight hours' notice. If you can, though, and there are a lot of different places in the world you would love to visit, a last-minute travel club that offers members close-out prices on unsold cruises, tours, resorts, and air tickets may be worth the price of admission ($20.00 to $48.00 a year).

Typically that fee will buy you access to a hotline telephone number with up-to-the-minute information on what travel bargains are available as well as a monthly newsletter. Have an unexpected long weekend coming up? The hotline might offer a five-day package tour to Acapulco for a 40 percent discount or round-trip air tickets to Las Vegas for half the lowest coach fare.

Among the last-minute clubs that operate nationally: *Worldwide Discount Travel*, 305-534-2082; *Entertainment Hotline Travel Club*, 800-828-0826; *Discount Travel International*, 800-334-9294. Recommended if you can leave from New York: *Moment's Notice*, 212-486-0503.

There is also a new "900" telephone service called *Last Minute Travel Connection* (900-446-8292; cost: $1.00 a minute) that offers anyone who calls a chance to buy last-minute discounted travel deals. A typical call will last five minutes or more, but there is no membership fee. When you call, you push telephone buttons to establish where you want to go, then listen to recorded messages about packages offered and where to call for further information.

▶ FLY AS A COURIER

If you can travel alone on a flexible schedule, the cheapest way to fly to many destinations in Europe, Asia, and South America is as a courier. Couriers have to make do with carry-on luggage, since their check-in baggage is supplied to them by a courier company. In return for a very low price on a round-trip ticket, couriers escort that baggage—usually business documents—from one airport to another. The day we called *Now Voyager*, a New York City–based courier booking agency (212-431-1616), we could have gotten a round-trip ticket from New York to Amsterdam or Copenhagen for $199 or a round-trip ticket to Singapore for $299. If you can leave at the very last minute, you can sometimes get a flight for as little as $50.00.

If being a courier intrigues you, call Now Voyager for more information or *Courier Travel Service* (516-374-2299). A book called *The Insider's Guide to Air Courier Bargains* by Kelly Monaghan ($16.95 from Inwood Training Publications, Box 438, New York, NY 10034) tells you everything you need to know about courier travel and includes a very complete directory of courier companies.

▶ ADD A VACATION TO THE END OF A BUSINESS TRIP

A very easy way to buy no-cost airline tickets is to switch from a direct route home on a business-class ticket to an alternate route with a stopover in a city you would like to visit. Instead of flying back to New York from San Francisco on a direct flight, you might find your ticket would buy you a San Francisco–Miami–New York or a San Francisco–Denver–New York route at an even lower price. Check your travel agent or call airlines direct.

▶ THROW AWAY PARTS OF PACKAGE DEALS

The big travel packagers buy at the best wholesale prices—charter airlines, hotels, restaurants, ground transportation, admission charges, etc.—and still make a profit even though they pass on some of the savings to you. Many people don't consider buying a package tour because they don't want to spend two weeks on a bus with a lot of potentially incompatible strangers. If you investigate certain packages carefully, however, you may discover you can throw away such elements as prepaid sightseeing buses and meals and still save money on what's left—usually airfare and accommodations.

▶ BUY DISNEY STOCK

This isn't a stock tip, although a lot of investing professionals think stock in the Walt Disney Company is a great buy. But if you own just one share of Disney (selling for about $38.00 when this edition went to press), you get free membership in *The Magic Kingdom Club* (for information, call 407-824-2600). Membership entitles you to discounts of up to 40 percent at some Disney resorts, plus discounts at stores and rides and even 10 percent off your airline tickets if you use Delta to get to Orlando.

If you buy only one share, your brokerage commission will probably exceed the price of your stock. And you'll have to wait three months or so after your stock purchase to exercise membership privileges. Nevertheless, if you're going to spend a week at a Disney resort with a family of four, this is a terrific deal.

▶ DON'T RESERVE USING A HOTEL-CHAIN 800 NUMBER

The central reservations office of any big hotel or motel chain will frequently quote a higher rate than the desk clerk at the specific place you want to stay. You can also often negotiate a reduced price with the desk clerk, but can't with the central office. The best idea is to first get rates from the central office (a free 800 call), then call the desk clerk to make your actual reservations.

▶ DELAY CAR RENTALS . . .

If you arrive at the airport late in the day and, except for the drive to your hotel, don't need a car until the next day, why not wait and rent it then? The cost of a shuttle bus or train is bound to be less than the cost of renting the car for a day, and you'll save garage expenses as well.

It works on the other end of the trip, too—why keep a car for an extra day if all you are going to do is drive it to the airport next morning?

▶ . . . BUT RESERVE ADVERTISED SPECIALS QUICKLY

When you see an ad for a special limited-time offer from a car-rental company, call and make your reservation at the special rate as quickly as you can. The companies change their rates frequently, and the special price may not be available in a day or two.

▶ TRY FOR NO-FEE TRAVELER'S CHECKS

There is absolutely no reason—other than a desire for excess profits—why issuers of traveler's checks must charge a fee for the service. After all, you are giving them ready cash. They, in return, are giving you checks that will not be cashed until sometime in the future. The income issuers make by investing your money during that "float" period is more than enough to earn them a handsome profit on an average transaction.

Depending on competitive pressures at the time of purchase, however, your bank may insist that a fee is necessary. If you keep a reasonable balance in a couple of accounts, ask them to waive the fee. If that fails, shop elsewhere. As this edition was going to press, American Express traveler's checks were available at some banks without fees, and Thomas Cook was issuing no-fee traveler's checks if they were cashed later at Thomas Cook offices.

▶ LIMIT YOUR USE OF TRAVELER'S CHECKS

When you use a traveler's check to pay a hotel, a restaurant, a car-rental agency, or just about anybody else when traveling abroad, you will nearly always be given an unfavorable exchange rate (which is why you'll usually get a delighted smile and a "yes" when you ask if your traveler's check will be accepted). Instead, use a credit card for all major expenses; the rate of exchange is usually quite good.

Cash your traveler's checks only at a bank or an office of the company that issues the checks, and pay only minor expenses with cash in the local currency.

▶ SWAP HOUSES—*VERY* CAREFULLY

This is an especially good way to save on large hotel bills if you are vacationing with children or as part of a group.

Or you may simply want to stay in one place for a while and have some extra space and cooking facilities.

We've never swapped houses ourselves, but have friends who have traded their condo in Hawaii for private houses or apartments in London, the south of France, and on two Caribbean islands. So far, they say, things have worked out very well. We suggest caution, and like the idea of dealing with a third party that arranges the trade, even though it will cost more than simply listing your house in a directory and working out the trade yourself.

Better Homes and Travel (30 East 33rd Street, New York, NY 10016; 212-689-6608) screens its home exchangers and makes preliminary arrangements for homes and villas in Europe, the Caribbean, and the United States. There's a nonrefundable $50.00 registration fee and quite a stiff fee (from $100 to as much as $500) if and when an exchange takes place.

There are also a couple of publishers (*Vacation Exchange Homes,* 800-638-3841; *Intervac Home Exchange,* 800-756-4663) who will list your home for a fee (about $50.00) in their directories. The listing describes your home and spells out what (and where and when) you are willing to swap it for. You may then get a call from someone or you may call listings that interest you. After a few calls and the exchange of photos and references, you may decide to swap.

If this sounds complicated, it is. And your chances of swapping are obviously better if you are offering a Hawaii condo or an East Side Manhattan apartment rather than a North Dakota farmhouse.

If you want to attempt a swap, start very early—at least six months ahead of time. Unless you are somewhat flexible about time and accommodations, your chances of success are probably slim. Nevertheless, it may be worth a try, especially if you decide to rent through BH&T if a swap doesn't materialize. They'll refund your $50.00 fee if you ultimately decide to rent through them.

▶ USE A HALF-PRICE COUPON BOOK

Entertainment Publications (800-477-3234; in MI 313-637-8400) sells a one-year membership in "Travel America at Half Price" for $32.95. You'll get a directory of more than 1,200 hotels and motels in the United States, Canada, and the Caribbean (including most of the major chains) and a membership card that will allow you to make advance reservations for rooms at a 50 percent discount off regular rates "subject to availability." In practice, that means you can't expect to get a discount at peak times when the hotels have rooms reserved at full rates.

The same company also publishes "Half-Price Europe" ($38.00) as well as more than ninety regional or single-city coupon books. Even if you never leave your own area, one of these ($25.00 to $40.00 each) can be a real money saver. If you plan on spending a week in another city, by all means consider buying a coupon book first. All of the books offer discounts of up to 50 percent and two-for-one deals on hotels, bed and breakfasts, restaurants, movies, theaters, sports attractions, retail stores, and tourist attractions.

The best restaurants in most areas don't participate, and there are annoying restrictions on when discounts are available. So most of the coupons will be wasted. But the four area books we have checked out all featured at least a couple of restaurants we wanted to visit, and that's all it takes to at least break even.

▶ USE A 25 PERCENT DISCOUNT CREDIT CARD

The typical restaurant two-for-one deal in an Entertainment Publications discount book (see above) gives you the lower priced of two entrees free. Cocktails, wine, appetizers, desserts, and coffee aren't included. Since the price of those items may exceed the price of the two entrees, it is easy to end up with a discount of less than 25 percent off the total restaurant bill.

The IGT Charge Card (800-444-8872 for a free brochure and list of participating restaurants nationwide) is an attractive alternative to the discount book concept. You use it just as you would any other credit card, charging the full price of your meal—all food, liquor, and wine—at any time, at any participating restaurant, as many times as you like. When your monthly statement comes, you are given a 25 percent discount exclusive of tips and taxes.

The IGT Charge Card's annual membership fee is $48.00, so you break even after spending $200 (as of this writing, first year membership was being offered free). As you would expect, few of the best restaurants in any area participate. Nevertheless, when we reviewed the list of participating restaurants, we were surprised to find one in our area that we had enjoyed a lot in a recent visit. We also spotted two restaurants in New York City and one in Los Angeles that we knew we liked and could visit in the next year. The IGT card made sense for us.

Although it claims "nationwide" participation, the IGT card is strongest in the New York metropolitan area and in Florida.

▶ CHECK ON INSURANCE COVERAGE BEFORE TRAVELING ABROAD

It could prove to be an expensive mistake if you aren't sure your automobile or health insurance will cover you in the country you are visiting. Call your agent and/or talk to your benefits administrator. If you plan to drive while in a foreign country, call the American Automobile Association (AAA) to see if you'll need an international driver's license. You might also ask—even if you aren't a member—about supplemental insurance.

▶ GET DISCOUNTS ON GREENS FEES

If you are planning a golfing vacation, or are a golfer who travels often, call the National Golfer's Association (800-347-4653) for information about membership benefits. Annual dues are currently $50.00, but the club has negotiated big discounts on greens fees at some good golf courses and also offers airline and hotel discounts that may be worth your while.

▶ EAT YOUR BIG MEAL AT LUNCH

The menus may be exactly the same, but the price of lunch at most of the world's restaurants is invariably cheaper—often by 30 to 40 percent—than dinner.

▶ GET DINNER FOR THE PRICE OF A DRINK

We have a young friend who has systematically investigated the different free cocktail-hour appetizers at some of San Francisco's best-known and, in some cases, most expensive hotels and restaurants. His favorite place charges an outrageously high price for drinks. But one glass of wine, he points out, can be sipped for the forty-five minutes it takes to eat what he considers quite a satisfying free six- or seven-course dinner. He strongly suggests you overtip if you like the place well enough to go back.

▶ EAT DINNER EARLY

In many restaurants, the difference between ordering the same dinner at 6:55 P.M. and 7:05 P.M. isn't just ten minutes. The earlier meal may be as much as 50 percent less expensive. Ask about "early bird" and pretheater specials when you call for reservations.

▶ GET PRICES ON SPECIALS

"Hello, my name is Dave. Let me tell you about our specials tonight." Too often, Dave skips one ingredient: the price. Knowing that most people are reluctant to ask their friendly waiter the price of specials, many restaurants overprice them. Ask before you order.

▶ TAKE HOME A FREE LUNCH

Until a few years ago, we were uncomfortable about asking for what is unfortunately called a "doggie bag." Then, as guests of a business associate during a wonderful dinner in New York City at Lutece, perhaps America's finest French restaurant, we watched a celebrity multimillionaire at the next table beam as his doggie bag was graciously handed to him. We haven't given it a second thought since.

▶ SKIP THE ENTREE

If you are a light eater or aren't very hungry, order two appetizers and ask that one of them be served as your main course. Appetizers are usually priced at less than a third of the cost of a main course.

▶ SHARE COURSES

In many restaurants, one salad order is more than large enough for two. In Italian restaurants, we usually share a pasta course. And we invariably share one dessert.

▶ BEFORE YOU GO TO NEW YORK . . .

With the ticket price of a new musical reaching $100, going to the theater in New York City has become prohibitively expensive for people who aren't on expense accounts. But there are ways to find bargains:

- *The Hit Show Club* (630 Ninth Avenue, New York, NY 10036; 212-581-4211) prints and distributes "two-fer" coupons that you can redeem at the box office for a third off many Broadway and some off-Broadway shows. Send a SASE at least three weeks before your trip to get current discount tickets before you leave. You can stay on the club's mailing list from then on, if you like. If you call the above number, you will get a recorded message telling you what shows are currently offering discounts.
- *TKTS booths,* operated by the Theater Development Fund, are located at Duffy Square (47th and Broadway) and 2 World Trade Center in Manhattan and in downtown Brooklyn at the intersection of Court and Montague streets. If you want to take a chance, you can go to one of these booths the day of the performance you want to attend and get half-price tickets (plus a $1.75

service charge). How good are your chances? Terrible for the hottest new shows, quite good for just about anything else, including many long-running hits.

- *The Theater Development Fund* (1501 Broadway, Suite 2110, New York, NY 10036) restricts its membership list, but the qualifications are loose enough for many, if not most, of us to qualify. You must be a teacher, student, union member, retired, a performing arts professional, or a member of the clergy or the armed services. After you write for an application (include SASE), return it with a $5.00 one-time fee. If you are accepted as a TDF member, you will get periodic, usually monthly, offerings of discounted tickets, usually in the $10.00 to $12.00 price range, for a wide range of shows and events. You can also purchase TDF "vouchers" for about $15.00, which are good for additional discounts (sometimes even free admission) to a variety of performing arts events. TDF often offers unique experiences, such as a ticket to a rehearsal of the New York Philharmonic for $5.00.

▶ BEFORE YOU GO TO WASHINGTON, D.C. . . .

Call your congressman's or senator's local office and get free passes to the White House and Senate and House galleries. The White House tour is more extensive than the one tourists stand in line to pay for.

▶ IF YOU'RE GOING TO NEW YORK, LOS ANGELES, OR SAN FRANCISCO . . .

Express Hotel Reservations (800-356-1123) is a discount reservation service that handles a number of hotels in these three cities, ranging in category from budget to deluxe. You should probably check out any other discount rates you may qualify for before calling them, but they say they offer the lowest prices available, whether for weekdays or weekends.

▶ UNDER 26?
GET A CIEE CARD

The Council on International Educational Exchange (CIEE) is a nonprofit organization whose primary goal is to develop student exchanges and foster international understanding. For young travelers, especially those planning to travel, work, or study abroad, the CIEE is also a great penny-pinching resource.

The CIEE issues three International Identity Cards that will pay for themselves many times over on a trip abroad: Student ($14.00; proof needed that you are 12 or over and a junior-high, high-school, college, university, or vocational-school student); Youth ($14.00; proof needed that you are between twelve and 26); and Teacher ($15.00; proof needed that you are a full-time faculty member at an accredited institution).

The cards offer different benefits, but all make you eligible for discounts on transportation (local mass transit as well as airlines and railroads), accommodations, tourist attractions, cultural events, etc. All also include sickness, accident, life, and emergency medical-insurance coverage as well as access to a 24-hour toll-free Traveler's Assistance Service.

Even if you aren't planning a trip abroad, if you are a teacher or under 26, it is worth your while to write the Council (205 East 42nd Street, New York, NY 10017) and request a free copy of *Travel!* This annual travel catalog also has some information about domestic travel discounts.

▶ CHECK OUT FARES
FROM COUNCIL TRAVEL

Council Travel is the travel division of the CIEE, and is a good place for any budget-minded traveler to check for discounted airfares, railroad passes, and low-cost accommodations and car rentals. Some, but not all, of their discounts are available to anyone, not just students. Even students, however, shouldn't take for granted that Council Travel rates are the lowest available. They are nearly always competitive, but you should compare them with other consolidators and charter operators as well as with special airline promotional fares.

Council Travel doesn't have an 800 number, but does have offices around the country, including Boston (617-266-1926), New York (212-661-1450), Washington, D.C. (202-337-6464), Atlanta (404-377-9997), Miami (305-670-9261), Chicago (312-951-0585), Minneapolis (612-379-2323), Austin (512-472-4931), Boulder (303-447-8101), Seattle (206-632-2448), San Francisco (415-421-3473), and Los Angeles (818-905-5777).

▶ STAY IN YOUTH HOSTELS

At any age, hostels, which offer dormitorylike rooms, are the lowest-cost way to spend a night unless you are a camper. Prices range from as low as $5.00 to $25.00, and accommodations range from primitive barracks to authentic castles. Many serve meals and have recreational facilities. There are many more hostels in Europe than in the United States, where there are about 225 American Youth Hostels. To stay at one of the more than 5,000 International Youth Hostels worldwide, you must first purchase an American Youth Hostel membership card ($25.00 for one year for anyone between 18 and 54; $15.00 for everyone else). Cards are available at any Council Travel office or from American Youth Hostels (AYH), Box 37613, Washington, D.C. 20013 (202-783-6161).

▶ OVER 50? JOIN THE AARP

See Chapter 10 for other reasons, but quick-and-easy travel discounts alone make the $5.00 annual membership fee to the American Association of Retired Persons a must for anyone over 50. Nearly all hotel and motel chains offer at least a 10 percent discount to AARP card holders. Some offer discounts as high as 50 percent. Car-rental and some restaurant chains also give AARP members discounts, as do individually owned motels, bed and breakfasts, and resorts.

Once you have an AARP card, get in the habit of always asking about a possible AARP discount when you make any kind of travel purchase. You will often be pleasantly surprised. But negotiate for the best deal possible first, and only then ask for your AARP discount.

▶ OVER 62? GET A 10 PERCENT DISCOUNT ON AIRFARE . . .

Some airlines give 62-and-over customers a 10 percent discount off their published fares. But they usually don't offer this discount on special promotional fares, which normally are more than 10 percent lower than regular fares. You won't get the discount if you buy from a consolidator, either. So always check out other alternatives before settling for just 10 percent off.

▶ . . . OR BUY AIRLINE SENIOR COUPON BOOKS

This is the best deal of all for seniors who enjoy traveling. Available from all major domestic airlines, you buy a book of four or eight coupons, each one good for a one-way coach seat anywhere the airline flies in the U.S. (usually except for Alaska and Hawaii, which require two coupons). Except on TWA, you even get credited for frequent-flier mileage when you use senior coupons.

As of this writing, a typical coupon when bought in a book of eight costs between $106 and $112. That may not make sense on a short-haul flight, but it is hard to beat on longer distances.

There are some differences in the airline programs. TWA allows you to buy a companion book for a somewhat higher price if you are traveling with someone under 62. Some airlines sell off-peak coupon books for a lower price than regular books. Some restrict travel to certain places to certain times of the week.

If you qualify for a senior coupon book, first consider where you want to go and which airline offers the best service to those places from your home airport. Call that airline and get complete information before you buy.

▶ OVER 55 AND A CONSTANT TRAVELER? FLY CONTINENTAL

As of this writing, Continental was the only airline offering a senior pass that gives you a maximum of one one-way ticket a week to and from anywhere in the U.S. for a year. The price is currently $1,799, you can buy a companion ticket for the same price, and you can fly anywhere in the U.S. If you fly more than eighteen times, that's less than $100 a ticket.

For $3,599 you can get a global pass (Continental flies to Europe, Australia, Mexico, and the Caribbean). There are also ways to pay extra to go abroad on a U.S. pass. There is some small print you should read and a few restrictions on both passes, but they could be great bargains if you love to travel and Continental stays in business for the year covered by your pass.

▶ OVER 62? STOP PAYING NATIONAL PARK FEES

You are now eligible for a free Golden Age Passport, which entitles you and a companion to free admission to any national park, monument, or historic site, as well as 50 percent off camping and user fees. There's a Golden Access Passport that gives disabled people the same free access.

▶ OVER 65? RIDE AMTRAK

You can get a 25 percent discount on one-way tickets. Call 800-872-7245 for information.

(See Chapter 4 for tips on shopping for travelers.)

7

Saving on Quality Clothing

An effort has been made throughout this book to offer money-saving tips that don't involve a lot of extra time or effort. But when it comes to shopping for clothing, there are not too many time-efficient ways to get the very best bargains. Most of those are found by people who don't mind spending hours checking on sales, love to read and compare catalogs, and can spend a full day at an outlet mall and then happily repeat the experience a week later.

If you hate to shop, you can still manage to save money with some of the tips in this chapter. Tips you will probably want to avoid are labeled FSO—For Shopaholics Only.

The revolution that has swept the retail world in the past decade has changed the way all of us shop for clothes. Many of the great department stores and traditional specialty stores that dominated the apparel scene for generations have disappeared. The survivors have had to adopt aggressive new selling strategies to hold on to old customers and attract new ones. The competition is fiercer than ever for your clothing dollar—among department stores, specialty stores, discount stores, off-price retailers, designer and factory outlet stores, mass merchandisers, mail-order sellers, and even wholesale clubs. The opportunities for bargain hunters have never been greater, but neither has the potential for confusion.

Fewer and fewer stores can be relied on completely for quality and for knowledgeable service. Those that can usually cater to people who can afford the best at any cost. When you shop anywhere else, including many traditional department and specialty stores that now stock merchandise they might once have shunned, it is important to know how to recognize quality and a proper fit.

Nowhere in this chapter will you find advice on saving money by buying inexpensively produced clothing. Our philosophy is simple: Cheap isn't cheap if you wear it once. Expensive isn't expensive if you wear it forever. The goal is to buy "expensive" for as little as possible.

▶ WHO DESIGNS DESIGNER LABELS?

Usually not the designer who has lent his or her name to the clothing label. In most cases, the rights to the name have been sold to a manufacturer who then pays a royalty, a percentage of the manufacturer's cost, to the designer.

With a few honorable and usually high-priced exceptions, a designer label is not a guarantee of quality. Three checklists in this chapter will help you avoid shoddy merchandise and spot a well-made garment. Use them no matter what the label is.

▶ DESIGNER VERSUS BRAND NAME VERSUS PRIVATE LABELS

If you suspect the industry may be out to confuse you on purpose, you aren't far wrong. What's in a label? Not much. Is Christian Dior, who died quite a few years ago, a designer label or a brand name? Certainly, in cases like this, you can at least be positive that Monsieur Dior himself had nothing to do with the hemline. Famous models and movie stars lend their names to labels, too, although this is usually seen mainly in mass merchandisers like K mart.

Private labels are one way department stores have fought back against their dependence on designer label clothing. If you know you may be able to buy a famous designer label cheaper at an off-price or designer outlet store, why buy at a department store? Realizing that too many people have come to this conclusion, many department stores have devoted a lot of their resources to establishing their own private labels.

Because department stores and specialty chains have so much at stake in their private labels, you will often find very good buys in quality clothing at certain stores. Stores as different as The Limited, Barney's, Neiman Marcus, and The Gap have developed private label lines that offer a consistent fit and a sense of fashion that reflects each store's image.

You should also know, however, that some private label apparel is bought from a manufacturer who may be selling exactly the same apparel to another department or specialty store in the same area. Only the labels will be different. *And the prices.* It is entirely possible that the same suit will cost $600 at a department store and $350 at a second-floor walk-up discount specialty store across town.

What to do? Use the kind of quality checklists you'll find in this chapter and shop around.

▶ SAVE 50 PERCENT! BUT IS IT ON SALE?

Not always. More and more often, whether you are shopping in a department store, an off-price store, a factory or designer outlet, a mass merchandiser, or a mail-order catalog, a "sale" is not a sale but a cynical marketing gimmick. "Originally $100, now $49.95" is meaningless if the garment was never bought by anyone for $100, and, in fact, gives the retailer a handsome markup at the $49.95 price.

Some states have laws against this kind of deception,

but there are few efforts to prosecute any but the most blatant abuses. When you see a price tag stating "suggested retail price $100.00, our price $39.95," your first thought should be: "Suggested by whom?"

Unfortunately, there are fewer and fewer retailers who don't resort at least occasionally to such tactics. If you want to save money as well as buy quality clothing, you simply have to know how to examine every prospective purchase.

▶ ARE THERE STILL BARGAINS IN TRADITIONAL DEPARTMENT STORES?

With all the different kinds of retailers now competing for your clothing dollar, are there still bargains available in traditional department stores? Absolutely, but usually only at certain times of the year.

Department stores sell seasonally. Because they anticipate what you will want to wear *next* season, you can't walk into a department store in the Northeast on a 98-degree day in August and expect to find a good selection of bathing suits or summer dresses. That's when winter coats and wool dresses are featured.

To make room for next winter's clothing, summer clothes are now routinely put on sale in traditional department stores at just about the time you may want to wear them, in June. And winter clothing, on sale everywhere in January, has in recent years been put on sale by nervous retailers even before Christmas.

▶ SHOP OFF-PRICE STORES

They won't have your size or the color you want. Some of the clothing will be marked "irregular" or "imperfect." Buttons may be missing, and a thread may be loose. Service is either bad or nonexistent. But you can't think of yourself as a penny pincher unless you at least look into off-price stores from time to time. Quality is uneven, but you can definitely find quality clothing, often with designer labels, at incredible prices—up to 80 percent off.

A Quick Quality Checklist for All Clothing

- Stitching. Small stitches usually mean longer-lasting apparel. Stitches should be neat, straight, and even, although in a very well-made garment slightly uneven stitches indicate hand-sewing, always an indication of quality.

- Seams should be flat. The seam formed where two pieces of fabric meet should be straight. Even slight puckering should be avoided.

- Puckering at darts (the short, stitched folds that make a garment fit more closely) also indicates lower quality.

- Patterns (stripes, plaids, checks) should "shake hands" at the seams. If two pieces aren't matched exactly, it is a sure sign of a poorly made garment.

- Armholes and shoulders of jackets should fit smoothly, without any wrinkles.

- Pockets should be large enough to use comfortably and should have reinforced stitching.

- Few cheap garments use 100 percent natural fiber fabrics, so an all-cotton men's shirt, for example, is probably well constructed. This isn't to suggest that a lot of quality clothing isn't made of synthetic fibers.

- Check the grain of the fabric. It is important that every garment be cut "on-grain," meaning that lengthwise yarns hang perpendicular to the floor and crosswise yarns at a perfect 90-degree angle. This is much easier to spot in a plaid or a stripe; if these are cut "off-grain," horizontal and vertical lines won't match. But no garment will hang well if cut slightly "off-grain." They are getting hard to find, but a knowledgeable salesperson or a good tailor can point out examples of how important the grain of the fabric is.

- Look for flaws and variations in the fabric, but remember that some are normal and desirable in some natural fabrics.

Off-price stores are where manufacturers dump slow sellers returned by traditional stores (nothing to do with quality), irregulars (defects are sometimes hard to find and usually nothing that affects wearability), and over-stock. When credit crunches hit and a manufacturer needs cash quick, first-run merchandise may also turn up in off-price stores.

You've got to be careful when you find a bargain in an off-price store. Seconds (more serious flaws) and irregulars (minor ones) are supposed to be marked, but that doesn't always happen. Sizes aren't dependable either; the garments may have been incorrectly sized originally and that's the only reason they're in the off-price store. Try everything on.

Finally, make sure you know what the return policies of the store are.

These are the leading off-price chains that we have found most likely to offer at least some quality clothing at very attractive discounts (phone numbers for "location nearest you" information):

Marshall's (800-MARSHAL). More than 400 stores nationwide. Men's, women's, children's clothing. Among labels you'll find from time to time: Calvin Klein, Perry Ellis, Armani, Anne Klein. A Marshall's twenty miles away may have quite a different mix of clothing.

Loehmann's (212-902-0800). More than seventy stores nationwide, and, with Filene's Basement, the originator of the off-price concept. Women's clothing only. You'll never find all sizes, colors, etc., but legendary buys are still possible here. More likely for sizes 4 and 6.

Filene's Basement (800-666-4045). More than thirty stores, still confined to the Northeast. Men's and women's clothing. Recent find: men's dress shirts with a Brooks Brothers label for $14.00.

T. J. Maxx (800-926-6299). More than 380 stores nationwide. Men's and women's clothing. Donna Karan, Anne Klein, Esprit, Armani. A bit younger, more stylish than Marshall's.

Bolton's (718-786-7777). More than twenty-five stores in the Northeast. Women's clothing only. Lower-priced

A Quick Quality and Fit Checklist for Women

■ When you try on a coat or jacket, bend your arms; the sleeves should still come to your wrists.

■ Do the shoulder pads stay in place? Take the jacket off and put it back on a couple of times. It's a tell-tale sign of a poorly constructed garment if you have to keep adjusting the shoulder pads.

■ Jacket lapels that seem to be pressed flat or are stiff should be avoided. Lapels should be soft and rounded and should spring back into shape after you crumple or squeeze them.

■ When trying on a coat, wear the bulkiest jacket or sweater you intend to wear under it. The armholes should still feel comfortably roomy.

■ Sit down when you try on a skirt. It should have enough room in it to avoid creases across the front from sitting.

■ Pleats in a skirt should hang smoothly, without parting at the hip area.

■ The waistbands of all types of skirts should fit snugly, but without any indication that they will roll.

■ No matter how they are finished (hand-rolled, blindstitched, etc.), hems on a well-made garment will fall smoothly, without any signs of unevenness, puckering, or rippling. Hems are easy to alter, though, so if everything else is okay, consider buying the garment.

■ Hemline stitches should always be invisible from the outside.

■ Zippers should be dyed to match the fabric and completely covered.

■ Buttons should be functional. Sticking a button on for decoration is a sign of cheap design. If buttons are supposed to match the color of the garment, they should match exactly.

■ No matter what you buy, make certain you can move easily while you have it on. "It looks great so I don't mind being uncomfortable" is never a successful long-term strategy.

manufacturers as well as brands like Evan Picone and designers like Anne Klein.

▶ SHOP DEPARTMENT-STORE CLEARANCE CENTERS

Some top-line department stores, including Nordstrom, Saks Fifth Avenue, and Neiman Marcus, ship unsold clothing from main stores to their own clearance centers. You won't find current-season clothing at these locations, but the quality is usually dependable and markdowns of up to 75 percent are possible.

▶ SHOP OFF-PRICE STORES AND EVERYWHERE ELSE [FSO]

Now let's discuss the tactics used by shopaholics. They don't "look into off-price stores from time to time." They haunt them. They make special trips to factory and designer outlet centers—and repeat the trip a couple of weeks later.

If you have guessed that we don't shop this way, you are right. But there's no question that those who do find the greatest bargains. And a true shopaholic loves the game.

The game involves such tactics as these:

- Visiting the store just before the announced sale day. Sometimes salespeople will bend the rules and allow early sale shopping. If not, the shopaholic locates every potential buy beforehand and is the first in line the morning of the sale.
- Being constantly on the lookout for clothing that isn't marked "as is," but has some easily correctable flaw (a missing button, a broken stitch, etc.). Shopaholics immediately ask for a much lower price. They also look for and, more often than you would imagine, find mismarked items—early in a sale, before the manager is aware of the mistake some harried clerk made. This is sheer shopaholic bliss.
- Getting to know clerks and managers at different stores

A Quick Quality and Fit Checklist for Men

- Make certain there is felt backing stitched under the collar of any suit or sports jacket.

- Zippers should be sewn in absolutely straight and should lie flat.

- Every well-made shirt has two rows of stitching under the arm-holes.

- Extra fabric often indicates quality, since the manufacturer isn't cutting close to save a few cents. There should be a minimum of ⅜ inch of fabric on both sides of the center seam in a pair of pants. Even if you don't need the extra length, be suspicious if a jacket doesn't have an inch or two of extra fabric under the cuff to allow for lengthening.

- The edges of fabric inside a jacket should be stitched. If you see a piece of fabric that looks like it could unravel, avoid the jacket.

- Buttonholes should be strongly reinforced with thread, and jacket buttonholes should have a slight "keyhole" effect on the lapel side. Buttons should button easily; if the hole is too small, it is a sign of a hastily made garment.

- Check to make sure the sleeve lining is neatly stitched to the jacket lining and the coat itself at the armpit. If it looks uneven or badly stitched, avoid the jacket.

- Squeeze the lapels for a couple of seconds. If they don't spring back to their original shape immediately, avoid the jacket.

- The waistbands of pants should be reinforced with a stiffening fabric inside the lining. All well-made pants also have a second button inside the fly on the left, just below the waist button, to ensure a better fit and relieve pressure on the waist button.

- Don't even bother to go into the fitting room if a jacket doesn't lie flat on your shoulders. This is nearly always extremely difficult to alter. So is the length of the jacket.

and calling from time to time about big ticket items. "Any change in the price of that suede coat you've never had on sale?"

- Getting on every mailing list possible and tracking prices in different catalogs.

▶ SHOP DESIGNER OUTLETS

Off-price stores are still a hit-or-miss proposition. You've got to be lucky, your timing has to be right, or you have to be a relentless repeat shopper. That's less true of the designer outlets now found throughout the country, usually off a main highway in small malls that include a number of designer and factory outlet stores. Ralph Lauren, Calvin Klein, Anne Klein, Liz Claiborne, and Harvé Bernard are among the leading designers who operate outlet stores, selling their clothing at discounts of up to 75 percent.

What's sold in these stores keeps changing, depending on economic conditions in the retail business. Originally, designer outlet stores were supposed to sell end-of-season leftovers that hadn't been shipped to department and full-price specialty stores. Troubled times for many traditional stores, however, have widened the assortment of newer apparel in many designer outlets. If the trend continues, some outlets are likely to have a very substantial assortment of their designer's newer apparel.

The clothing in most of these stores is prime quality, although some also include clearly marked seconds and irregulars. Unlike the off-price stores, most are well furnished and are pleasant places to shop. It is a good idea to know beforehand what the designer label clothing is selling for in department and full-price specialty stores. As designer outlets have become more popular, prices have tended to rise. Not everything is necessarily a great bargain or even a good buy.

Because of agreements with traditional retailers, you won't see any ads for these stores. New malls are being built every month. For a list of locations of established malls where you will find some (never all) of the designers mentioned above, as well as others, see next page.

Major Designer Outlet Mall Locations

Northeast and Mid-Atlantic:

NEW YORK: Central Valley, Cohoes, Lake George, Latham, Monticello, Niagara Falls, Plattsburgh, Saratoga, Watertown. NEW JERSEY: Flemington, Secaucus, Shrewsbury. PENNSYLVANIA: Lancaster, Reading, York. MARYLAND: Annapolis, Perrysville, Queenstown. DELAWARE: Rehoboth. MAINE: Freeport, Kittery. NEW HAMPSHIRE: Keene, North Conway, West Lebanon. VERMONT: Manchester. MASSACHUSETTS: Buzzards Bay, Fall River, Lawrence, Lenox, New Bedford, Plymouth. CONNECTICUT: Branford, East Windsor, Milford, Mystic, Norwalk.

South and Southwest:

VIRGINIA: Prince William, Virginia Beach, Waynesboro, Williamsburg. WEST VIRGINIA: Martinsburg. TENNESSEE: Chattanooga, Pigeon Forge. NORTH CAROLINA: Blowing Rock, Burlington, Smithfield. SOUTH CAROLINA: Hilton Head, Myrtle Beach, Santee. GEORGIA: Commerce. FLORIDA: Orlando, Sarasota, West Palm Beach. ALABAMA: Boaz, Foley. TEXAS: Conroe, El Paso, Hillsboro, New Braunfels, Sulphur Springs.

Midwest:

OHIO: Aurora, Sandusky. INDIANA: Michigan City. ILLINOIS: St. Charles. WISCONSIN: Appleton, Kenosha. MICHIGAN: Birch Run, Holland, Monroe. MISSOURI: Branson, Osage Beach.

West and Far West:

ARIZONA: Sedona. CALIFORNIA: Barstow, Cabazon, City of Commerce, Eureka, Folsom, Gilroy, Lake Tahoe, Monterey, Pacific Grove, Vacaville. COLORADO: Durango, Silverthorne. WASHINGTON: Burlington. OREGON: Lincoln City. MONTANA: Billings. WYOMING: Jackson. SOUTH DAKOTA: Rapid City.

▶ SHOP FACTORY OUTLETS

A step down in chic from designer outlets, factory outlets are nevertheless a good place to bargain hunt for clothing and footwear. The first factory outlets were actually attached to the factories and sold seconds, damaged goods, and irregulars. Because these factories were usually in the old textile and leather centers on the East Coast, the factory outlet phenomenon was limited to that part of the country until quite recently.

What happened, of course, is that factory outlets became so profitable that manufacturers opened new stores and started producing perfectly sound, first-line merchandise for them. There are now factory outlets nationwide, many of them grouped into outlet centers. There are also quite a few retail operations that try to pass themselves off as factory outlets, but are usually just discounters of second-rate merchandise.

Long-standing agreements between manufacturers and regular retail customers, although under some pressure these days, make it unlikely that you will find the very newest lines or fashions in factory outlets. But a lot of good quality merchandise is sold in them. As with designer outlets, it helps to know beforehand the normal retail sale price of an item you might buy in a factory outlet; too often, there is little difference or the outlet is actually more expensive. The outlets of some manufacturers are more dependable than others, and you will get a sense of this as you spend time in them.

If you have never visited a large factory outlet center, be prepared to be somewhat overwhelmed by the number of stores and the variety of the merchandise offered. If you are fairly close to one, you might want to devote a first trip mainly to looking around and eliminating stores you know you aren't interested in. Then go back and shop the others.

Many outlet centers are located in vacation or resort areas, and you might want to know about them if you are planning a trip. You can get a booklet with helpful information on more than 275 outlet centers nationwide by sending a check for $5.95 to *Joy of Outlet Shopping,* Box

Questions to Ask Before You Buy Anything

- Would I like this just as much if the label read "Sears" instead of "Famous Designer"?

- Do I really believe I'll be able to wear this next year . . . five years from now?

- Is this garment well made enough to last that long?

- How much will dry cleaning cost?

- Am I prepared to wash and iron this every time I wear it?

- Does it really fit, or am I tempted to buy it because it fits pretty well and is a size smaller than I usually buy?

- How does this fit into my wardrobe? What can I wear it with that I own now?

- What else will I have to buy to make full use of this garment? Will I need special accessories? Do I really want to spend that much more?

- Where will I be able to wear this—given my actual (as opposed to my fantasy) life-style?

- Does it go with the coat I intend to wear it with? If it is a coat, does it coordinate with everything else I own?

- Can I use this year round if I add or subtract a layer? If it is a one-season garment, ask once again where and when you can wear it. Do you go there/do that in summer/winter?

- Am I at least fairly confident I've shopped enough elsewhere to be sure this is a good value?

17129, Clearwater, FL 34622. The booklet tells you where every one of the nation's outlet centers is located and what its hours are. It also lists the stores in each center and tells you what kind of merchandise and discounts you are likely to find in more than 420 outlet chains.

▶ BUY AND SELL AT CONSIGNMENT SHOPS

A number of readers of the first edition wrote to tell us how well they do buying and selling clothes at consignment shops. The best consignment shops buy only good quality used clothing that is still in style and in excellent condition. When an article of clothing is sold in the shop, the original owner typically gets 40 to 50 percent of the sale price.

Although some women use consignment shops only to sell clothing they no longer want, many sellers are also regular buyers. You can find top designer-label clothing in many consignment shops, often at a small fraction of original prices. And once you become a regular customer, some shops will call to tell you when something special turns up in your size.

▶ SHOP IN BAD WEATHER [FSO]

Store managers get lonely during a snowstorm at the end of January or on the hottest day in August. Those are particularly good shopping months in any case, but if you are one of the few customers in sight on a bad day and are serious about buying something, ask about the price tag. On-the-spot markdowns are possible.

▶ BEWARE THE 90 PERCENT DISCOUNT

For as long as world-famous designers have shown their new collections at openings attended by the rich and the high-fashion elite, there have been frantic efforts starting the next day to copy the new line by manufacturers who have no intention of paying the designer a penny.

This is perfectly legal. "Knock-offs" are an accepted part of the industry. In fact, many designers "knock off" their own high-priced designs in lower-priced lines of clothing, using less expensive fabrics and mass production methods but still producing good quality garments.

What is not legal is counterfeiting, which is putting a fake label in a copy of an item of apparel or an accessory and then selling it as the real thing. In addition to being illegal, a counterfeit is nearly always a shoddily produced piece of merchandise.

If you see a $500 Gucci bag for $39.95 and think it is too good to be true, it is.

▶ BUY "SLIGHTLY IMPERFECT" HOSIERY BY MAIL

So slight are the imperfections in the hosiery we've seen ordered from the *Hanes L'Eggs "Showcase of Savings"* catalog that we'd probably use it even if it didn't offer an unconditional 100 percent money-back guarantee. With that guarantee, and the opportunity to save 50 percent on the brand we use (all the popular Hanes brands are available), the catalog is a basic annual resource. For a free catalog, write: Showcase of Savings, L'Eggs Brands, Inc., P.O. Box 1010, Rural Hall, NC 27098-1010.

If you prefer No Nonsense brands of pantyhose, they also offer "practically perfect" hosiery at 50 percent to 60 percent off retail prices. For a free catalog, write: *No Nonsense Direct*, Box 26095, Greensboro, NC 27420-6095.

▶ CHECK OUT SPIEGEL'S CATALOG

Spiegel (800-345-4500) is a mail-order giant, but its clothing seems to be a cut or two above the competition's in terms of fashion. The big Spiegel catalog ($3.00, money back with first order) includes much more than clothing; it is a good resource to check in other areas as well. Spiegel publishes sales catalogs regularly and has a deserved reputation for service.

BUY MEN'S DRESS SHIRTS BY MAIL

Paul Frederick Shirt Company (140 W. Main St., Fleet-wood, PA 19533; 215-944-0909) is a manufacturer of quality shirts that you will find in better stores with designer or store labels. The same shirts are available direct from the company for discounts that can be as high as 50 percent off store prices. Send $1.00 check or money order for a catalog.

▶ BUY FROM "THE UNDERWEAR KING"

That's how *D & A Merchandise Company* (22 Orchard St., New York, NY 10002; 212-925-4766) bills itself. Most name brand lingerie and underwear (men's and women's) at average savings of 25 to 35 percent. Prices quoted by phone or by return letter with SASE; the catalog is $2.00.

▶ BUY FROM LANDS' END OR L. L. BEAN

There are other good general mail-order catalogs, but we continue to find these two the most reliable for both men's and women's casual clothing. Discounts off retail prices can't be quoted because you won't find this clothing in retail outlets, but savings of from 20 to 35 percent off comparable apparel are likely.

Once you are on their mailing lists and buy even occasionally, you'll get seasonal catalogs. Both feature a few pages of marked down, discontinued merchandise at very large discounts off previous prices. We nearly always find something to buy, and have never been disappointed.

Lands' End (800-356-4444); *L. L. Bean* (800-221-4221)

▶ RENT INSTEAD OF BUYING

Want a knock-'em-dead evening dress for a once-in-a-lifetime occasion? At least check on what's available at rental shops in your area. Typically, you might spend as much as $200 to rent a $2,000 dress, and the odds get better every day that you won't be the only one at the affair with a money-saving secret. Check the Yellow Pages under "formal wear."

▶ MAKE A BUYER'S TRIP TO NEW YORK CITY [FSO]

Although not much clothing is actually manufactured in New York anymore, it is still the capital of the garment industry and a must stop for retail buyers from everywhere in the country. You can't get into the wholesale showrooms the buyers do, but savvy city shoppers know that not all of them are "for the trade only." The *Bargain Hotline,* 540-0123, is updated weekly (on Friday nights) and lists upcoming sample and overstock sales in garment center showrooms—complete with what kind of merchandise is on sale at each showroom, their addresses, and information about what kind of payment will be accepted.

The number can only be dialed from a phone within the New York metropolitan area (212, 516, 718, and 914 area codes) and the call will cost $1.95 for the first minute, 75 cents a minute after that.

If you are a true shopaholic who lives in the New York area or visits it frequently, you might want to subscribe to the *S&B Report* (212-679-5400), a $45.00-a-year newsletter that lists between 50 and 250 different New York City designer showroom sales each month, complete with addresses, sales dates and hours, and a description of the merchandise. Claimed savings on current designer lines: 50 to 70 percent off retail prices.

▶ BUY MATERNITY CLOTHES BY MAIL

Mother's Place (800-829-0080) doesn't offer discounts, but it does offer a free catalog of its own label maternity clothing at very attractive prices.

▶ BUY KIDS' CLOTHES BY MAIL

Olsen Mill Direct (800-537-4979) sells the Osh-Kosh line of children's clothing at factory-outlet prices. The catalog is $2.00, money back with first order.

Sears (800-366-3000) and *JC Penney* (800-527-7889) sell clothing for everyone, of course, but their prices on kids' clothes are especially hard to beat.

▶ DON'T JUST BUY CLOTHES, PLAN A WARDROBE

Impulse shopping in clothing stores is as dangerous as it is in supermarkets. To get the most from your clothing dollar year after year, you must discipline yourself. Certain styles of clothes and colors look good on you; stick to them. Never buy anything unless you can coordinate it within your basic wardrobe. A pair of shoes that go with only one dress or a shirt that goes with only one sports jacket are expensive mistakes.

The best way to avoid impulse shopping for clothes is to make up a very definite list of what you need. Keep this list in a small notebook that you can always carry with you, and update it constantly. It may be months before you find exactly the summer jacket you are looking for, but if you have a coordinated wardrobe it may be worth the wait.

See page 140 for a list of questions to ask yourself before you make a final purchase decision on any garment or accessory. If you keep them in mind, you'll avoid a lot of mistakes.

▶ DON'T JUST BUY CLOTHES, INVEST IN THEM

If you always buy clothes to become part of an evolving but carefully coordinated wardrobe, you will need fewer items than if you buy the latest fashion fads or follow short-term trends. You will begin to think in terms of investing in clothes, not just buying them. While few of us can afford the very finest quality for every item in our wardrobe, investing in a few classic garments that fit that description becomes a realistic strategy.

You will seldom find the best for sale under signs that proclaim "60 percent off," but the exclusive specialty men's and women's stores that carry such merchandise all have sales, too. Look for their often sedate sale ads and stop in. There are clothing bargains at every price level, and the most satisfying in the long run may be the ones that were initially the most expensive.

▶ WORRY ABOUT BUTTONS

What happens if you lose one of the seven unusual buttons that "makes" the outfit? Try to buy an extra button or two with the garment.

Alternatively, what if you find a quality garment ruined only by cheap buttons? It often pays to buy the garment anyway, and purchase top-grade horn or natural buttons elsewhere.

▶ REMEMBER "DRY CLEAN ONLY" COSTS EXTRA

A woman who dresses for an executive job in a city office fifty weeks of the year can easily spend $1,500 a year on dry cleaning. Buying some clothes that need to be dry cleaned is unavoidable, but searching out summer blouses that can be washed is worth the effort.

As for clothes that must be dry-cleaned, avoid silk, because it is the most expensive fabric to have dry-cleaned as well as the most delicate, and pleated skirts and dresses of any fabric, because most dry cleaners will charge extra to press each pleat.

▶ LEAVE A NOTE FOR YOUR DRY CLEANER

If you know what caused a stain (even if you think it is obvious), pin a note over it when you send the garment to your dry cleaner. Helping him choose certain solutions and avoid others can make all the difference.

▶ USE A SPRAY TIE PROTECTOR

Men who dress in a suit and tie every day often find themselves spending hundreds of dollars a year on what they wrap around their necks. Few have not had the experience of buying a $30.00 tie and seeing it destroyed at lunch the next day by an errant drop of sauce. The new spray tie protectors actually work. Try a can on a couple of your favorites.

One more tip: If you water spot a silk tie, wait for it to dry and then simply rub the spot with another part of the tie. Nine times out of ten, you'll remove the spot.

▶ USE "SHOE GOO" ON KIDS' SNEAKERS

After a couple of months, an otherwise perfectly good pair of sneakers may begin to wear out in just one or two small areas of the sole. Instead of throwing them away, repair them overnight using an inexpensive tube of "Shoe Goo," available in most sporting-goods and many hardware stores. You can easily triple the life of a pair of sneakers this way.

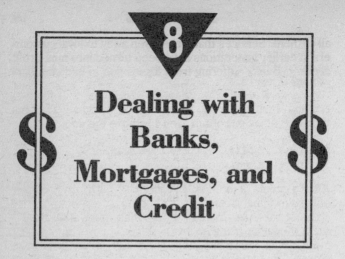

Dealing with Banks, Mortgages, and Credit

All of the services offered by your bank, credit card company, and any other kind of lender are considered "products" by these organizations. Just like cans of soup on a supermarket shelf, these financial products—from checking accounts and home equity loans to trust services and annuities—are conceived, priced, and marketed to make a profit.

Some people have trouble accepting this. After all, they trust their banks with their money, with their most precious and valuable documents if they have a safe deposit box, and with their complete financial histories if they take out a loan. Banks have grave fiduciary responsibilities that make them more than mere marketers of different financial products.

While this is true, and true that banks are subject to strict regulation by both state and federal laws and agencies, it is also a fact that banks must make a profit to survive, and the past few years have been hard on nearly all of them. Services that were given away to loyal customers in earlier generations have been turned into mini-profit centers. Banks suffering from losses due to bad commercial loans are under enormous pressure to make their retail consumer operations more profitable.

To put it bluntly, your friendly 1990s banker is likely to do anything legal to part you from as much of your money as possible. You can't protect yourself against some abuses. All banks, for instance, make you wait longer than is actually necessary to draw on a check deposited into your account. If you can imagine how much they earn a year by having the use of billions of dollars for an extra day or two, you can understand why.

Keep these three principles in mind when dealing with banks, other lenders, credit card organizations, and other credit-granting organizations (department stores, auto dealers, etc.):

- Don't pay interest on a loan unless you have to. *The best way to earn 12 percent tax-free on your money is to pay off any 12 percent loans you have outstanding.* With the exception of a home mortgage and perhaps loans to start a business or invest in an education, it is always better (barring the return of double-digit inflation) to save first, then spend.
- Take advantage of the competition between banks and between credit card organizations for your business. Shop around for the best deals you can get. A long-term relationship with one bank can be of some importance, but in these days of impersonal, computer-driven banking it doesn't mean as much as it once did.
- Learn a few basics about how interest rates on loans are calculated. (Tips in this chapter will help.) Most importantly, make sure you understand all the fine print in a loan or credit agreement before you sign it.

▶ KEEP SHOPPING FOR BETTER BANKING DEALS

Differences in geography, state laws, and changing competition within markets make it difficult to set minimum standards that can be applied to all the different kinds of checking accounts available. But the easiest way for banks to increase profits from their retail operations is to raise the fees and minimum balance requirements of current customers. At the same time they are doing this, they may be advertising special introductory deals to attract new accounts. That's why it's a good idea to read the ads from different banks about minimum balances, fees, and services. At least once a year, make sure you review what you are paying versus what's offered elsewhere.

This isn't to suggest that you continually switch banks to save a dollar a month or to escape an extra $1,000 minimum requirement. But if you let your bank take your business for granted, they will. When you do see a much better deal elsewhere, get the details and show them to an officer of your current bank. Every bank gives its officers at least some flexibility to make fee and other concessions to good customers. If you are one of them, your bank won't want you to leave.

▶ COMBINE ACCOUNTS AT ONE BANK

The best way to eliminate most fees and become the kind of customer a bank wants to keep happy is to deposit enough money to be perceived as a significant customer. That may mean trading off an extra percentage point or so of interest on a couple of thousand dollars, keeping it in a bank's federally insured money market deposit account, for instance, instead of a higher-paying money market mutual fund.

Keeping that kind of money in such an account will usually mean you won't need a minimum balance in your regular or NOW (Negotiable Order of Withdrawal, meaning interest-paying) checking account to escape fees. Since the very first rule of saving and investing is to have a minimum of three months' salary readily available for emergencies, a bank money market account makes good sense.

Another way to eliminate fees and become a more significant customer is to establish an IRA (Investment Retirement Account) with your bank. Many banks will now include IRA balances when determining what kind of deal you'll get on your checking account. It is perfectly legal to have more than one custodian for your IRA funds, so it is possible to keep just a portion at your bank.

▶ SHOP FOR THE BEST CD RATES

Before you buy or renew a Certificate of Deposit at your bank, check its rates against the competition by calling Bankquote Online (800-325-3242). It is easy to purchase a federally insured CD by mail, and rates vary significantly in different parts of the country.

▶ DON'T BUY CHECKS FROM YOUR BANK

Banks that once supplied good customers with free checks now mark up the checks they sell you by at least 100 percent, and sometimes 200 percent or more, over the price they pay their printers.

Deal direct with specialized check printers. All they need is a sample check from you (write "canceled" on it before mailing) to match any bank's necessary computer codes. Among reputable sources to contact for catalogs and prices: *Checks in the Mail Inc.*, 800-733-4443; *Current*, 800-533-3973.

▶ USE DIRECT DEPOSIT FOR YOUR SALARY CHECK

Not only is it a waste of time to stand in endless bank lines every week or two, you also get the use of your money faster when the company you work for sends your salary check to your bank electronically. If your employer offers direct deposit, have your salary deposited automatically into a money market or interest-bearing account.

▶ THE PENNY-PINCHER'S MORTGAGE

Unless you are certain you will own your home for only a few years and want to take a chance on changing interest rates, the best way to finance it is with a conventional fixed-rate mortgage amortized over as few years as possible. Since most people do sell their homes before the mortgage is paid off, make sure you or your accountant includes the points and origination fees in your calculations. A loan with a quarter-point higher rate might be preferable to a loan with high up-front costs.

ARMs (Adjustable Rate Mortgages) are dangerous; they shift the risk of interest rate changes from the lender to you. Don't listen to expert opinions: *No one* knows which way interest rates are headed in the future. Our opinion is that if you can't afford a fixed-rate mortgage, you probably can't afford the house. But if you are considering an ARM, make sure you work up a worst-case scenario to see what you would be faced with if interest rates go sky-high. And make doubly certain you understand all of the small print in an ARM agreement.

Why pay off your mortgage as quickly as you can? Few people ever calculate just how much more interest is involved in longer-term loans. Here's one example, using a fixed-rate mortgage of $100,000 at 10 percent:

	15-year loan	25-year loan	30-year loan
Monthly payments	$1,074.61	$ 908.70	$ 877.57
Amount owed after:			
5 years	$ 81,317	$ 94,164	$ 96,574
10 years	50,597	84,561	90,938
15 years	PAID	68,762	81,664
20 years		42,768	66,406
25 years		PAID	41,303
30 years			PAID
Total Amount Paid:	$ 193,429	$ 272,610	$ 315,926
Total Interest Paid:	$ 93,429	$ 172,610	$ 215,926

The $197.04 difference in monthly payments between a fifteen-year and a thirty-year loan is significant to anyone with a $100,000 mortgage. But so is the $122,497 difference in the amount of interest paid. And if you can manage just another $31.13 in payments (the difference between twenty-five-year and thirty-year loans), you'll save $43,316 and be able to burn the mortgage agreement five years sooner.

For most people, most of the time, paying the highest monthly payments possible for the shortest period of time possible is a sound investment decision.

▶ RENEGOTIATE YOUR MORTGAGE

As a general rule, it pays to look into refinancing if you plan to stay in your house for a minimum of five years and if the rate on your current mortgage is two percentage points or more above the going rate for a thirty-year fixed mortgage.

Depending on where you live, prevailing conditions, and the competition among mortgage lenders, you may have to pay up to 4 to 5 percent of the amount borrowed in up-front points and closing costs. Your present lender certainly isn't going to encourage you to cancel a loan whose terms are now very favorable to him. On the other hand, if your lender is convinced you are going to shop elsewhere, he may want to give you an attractive deal since he already knows you are creditworthy.

Here's an easy way to figure out how long it will be before it pays off to refinance. Just substitute your own numbers for those used in this example:

Suppose your present thirty-year $150,000 mortgage at 12 percent has a principal balance of $140,127 after exactly ten years. Your monthly payment is $1,543. It will cost you $3,500 in up-front points and penalties to refinance a twenty-year mortgage at 10 percent. Your new principal amount will be $143,627 ($140,127 + $3,500) and your new monthly payment $1,386. The numbers look like this:

Mortgage balance	$140,127
Plus points and penalties	+ 3,500
Total new mortgage principal	$143,627
Present monthly payment	$ 1,543
New monthly payment	− 1,386
Difference	$ 157

$3,500 refinancing costs
divided by $157 = 22.3 months.

If it takes 22.3 months before you pay off the cost of points and penalties, after that you will be saving the full $157 a month difference in monthly payments for the life of the mortgage. Total savings: $157 × 217.7 months (12 months × 20 years minus 22.3 months) = $34,179.

▶ PREPAY YOUR MORTGAGE PRINCIPAL

If you bought your home when interest rates were high, and interest rates are lower as you read this, prepaying your mortgage or adding to your monthly principal payments can make a lot of sense. Suppose you have a thirty-year fixed-rate mortgage of $200,000 at 11 percent. Your monthly payment is $1,904.65 and you will pay a whopping $485,674 in interest charges over the thirty-year life of the loan.

Now suppose that, after five years, you raise your monthly payment to $2,000 a month, instructing the lender to apply the $95.35 difference to the principal of the loan. You can always change your mind when you voluntarily make such prepayments. But if you continue to make that relatively small extra payment, it will mean a saving of $75,674 in total interest charges and your mortgage will be paid off nearly five years early.

One last calculation: If, instead of making that regular prepayment after five years, you saved $95.35 a month at 6½ percent interest, tax free, for the next twenty years, you would have only about $45,000 in total savings.

An accountant can help you factor in all the variables that pertain to you, including the deductibility of mortgage interest on your income tax. But, for many people, there is no better way to save money.

▶ STOP OVERPAYING INTO YOUR MORTGAGE ESCROW ACCOUNT

Millions of homeowners are paying more into escrow than they should, according to a recent joint investigation by the attorneys general of seven states. What this means is that your bank or whoever else holds your mortgage may unfairly be getting the use of money on which you could otherwise be earning interest. Even when, by state law or bank policy, interest is paid on an escrow account, the rate is never competitive with current money market rates.

The laws governing escrow accounts are murky, but it is worthwhile to fight back if you believe your mortgage holder is withholding more escrow than necessary to meet the costs of your real estate taxes and (sometimes) homeowner's insurance. Here's what to do:

- Read your mortgage agreement. See how much of a cushion (the lowest monthly balance in your escrow account in a year's worth of mortgage statements) the agreement allows your bank. Sometimes it is a month, sometimes two, sometimes none, and sometimes it isn't even mentioned.
- Check your mortgage statements month by month for at least the past twelve months. Each of the statements will tell you what your "ending escrow balance" is for that month. If your mortgage agreement allows no cushion, the lowest of those monthly balances should be just a few dollars. Even if your mortgage agreement didn't spell out the cushion allowed, you should be extremely unhappy if it is more than one-sixth of the yearly disbursements from the account. In other words, if the lender is paying $3,000 a year to cover your tax and insurance expenses, your monthly escrow balance should never be larger than $500. If it is more than one-

sixth higher (that's a two-month cushion), complain to the lender. Make it clear you'll take your complaint to your state's attorney general's office or bank authority. You stand a very good chance of getting a reduction in your monthly escrow bill.

▶ GET RID OF HIGH-INTEREST CREDIT CARD DEBT

Probably the worst sin a penny pincher can commit is to get in the habit of using credit cards as a way to borrow money. The rates are exorbitant—typically 16 to 21 percent—and the temptation to keep adding to the principal amount gets millions of people in real trouble every year.

The only smart times to use credit cards are when (1) you can't save money by paying cash; (2) you want to have recourse to a third party—the credit card company—to guard against the possibility of a merchant not delivering as promised; and (3) as a way to take advantage of the "float"—the period of time between the date of purchase and when you have to pay the credit card company the full amount in order to avoid any interest payments.

If you are carrying credit card debt, get rid of it as fast as you can. If necessary, and if you also have other high-interest debt such as a car loan, visit your bank or credit union and talk about one new "consolidator" loan at a lower rate that will enable you to pay off all your higher-interest debt. Homeowners can do this with home equity loans, a particularly good deal because interest payments on home equity loans are still fully tax deductible. Just remember that you are putting your home up as collateral.

▶ GET A FREE REVIEW OF YOUR CREDIT RATING

Until very recently, you couldn't get a look at the credit reports maintained on you by credit bureaus without paying them a fee. One of the major bureaus, TRW, will now send you a free copy of your report once a year. Many, if not most, credit reports have erroneous information in them. Especially if you are applying for a new mortgage or considering another major loan, it is a good idea to insist that any negative errors be corrected. To request a free report, write TRW, National Consumer Relations Center, 12606 Greenville Avenue, Box 749029, Dallas, TX 75374.

▶ IN TROUBLE? GET HELP

It's easy enough to give advice about staying out of trouble with credit card and other debt, but if you think you are already there, get help immediately. *The National Foundation for Consumer Credit* (800-388-2227) has regional offices that offer credit counseling.

▶ ESTABLISH YOUR KIDS' CREDIT RATINGS EARLY

Robert Dodd, a *Penny Pinching* reader in Houston, Texas, wrote to suggest that a good credit rating can lower interest expenses on a loan. He got several bank and department store credit cards in the names of each of his children when they were in their early teens and used the cards to make a few family purchases, always repaying promptly. By the time one of the young Dodds was ready to finance a first car in his own name, he had a six- or seven-year credit history with an A+ rating.

Mr. Dodd, obviously a realist, points out that your children never have to have access to the credit cards during their early teenage years. The only danger we see is that if your kids are not as responsible as the Dodds when they begin to borrow on their own, a good credit rating would make it a lot easier for them to get into trouble.

▶ THINK TWICE ABOUT "AFFINITY" CREDIT CARDS

Millions of people feel good about their Visa or Master-Card credit cards because they know that, by using it, they are helping their favorite charity or their college alma mater. The fact is, though, that very little money actually ends up with the affinity organization and you can nearly always get a better deal on the card elsewhere. Besides, whatever donation you are making isn't tax deductible. Write a check to your favorite cause instead.

▶ THE PENNY PINCHER'S BANK CREDIT CARD

For reasons already mentioned, we make certain that we always pay the full balance due each month on our Visa card as well as at the department stores where we maintain accounts. If we were to make a major purchase that meant we had to borrow money, we would go to our bank beforehand and get a loan from them. Under no circumstances would we even consider borrowing money by paying the high monthly carrying charges of most bank and department store cards.

This means we don't *care* how high the interest rates on our card are set. Instead, we choose a card that (1) has no membership fee; (2) offers a twenty-five-day grace period from the time of billing until payment is due; (3) offers some valuable supplemental benefits.

We've switched, dropped, and added cards over the past few years but always keep those three features in mind. To us, a bank credit card is both a great convenience (it is easier to account for expenditures by budget category this way than by keeping track of cash expenditures) and a way to postpone putting out cash for from thirty to forty-five days (and thus get the interest on that money ourselves).

On the other hand, before most purchases we ask how much we can save by paying cash. Green is quickly substituted for plastic when we like the answer.

What would we do if we were just starting out, couldn't get a low-interest bank loan, and had to buy a few high-ticket items before we had the ready cash to pay for them? First we would put off buying anything that wasn't absolutely necessary. Then we would pay the membership fee, if necessary, for a *second* bank card. Our first card, especially since it had no membership fee, might charge a high interest rate on unpaid balances. This second card would charge the lowest interest rates available. We would then use this second card *only* for the high-ticket items. Each month thereafter we would pay off as much as possible of the principal owed until we had no debt left. Finally, we would cut the card in two and hope never to use it again.

The Bankcard Holders of America, 560 Herndon Parkway, Suite 120, Herndon, VA 22070, offers a list of no-fee cards for $1.50. *Barron's* (a weekly financial newspaper) and *Money* magazine (a monthly) both list credit cards with the current lowest APRs (annual percentage rates) in each issue.

▶ THE FREQUENT FLIER'S CREDIT CARD

For most credit-card users, we stand by the pay-no-annual-fee strategies outlined in the previous tip. But if you travel by plane with some frequency, you should consider paying the annual membership fee necessary (as of this writing) to get a card that credits you with frequent-flier miles when you use it.

Competition among cards and airlines may change things, but as this edition was going to press these were the options:

- Every major airline except Delta sponsors a MasterCard or Visa card. For every dollar you charge on the card, you are credited with one mile in the airline's frequent-flier program. Choose the card sponsored by the airline you fly most frequently. The combination of miles earned that way and miles earned on the card can add up quickly.
- *American Express* card holders are credited with one mile per dollar charged and you can choose from seven different participating airlines when you cash the mileage in. American Express charges an extra fee to members who sign up for the program (currently, the first year fee is waived) and—an even bigger catch— you must charge a minimum of $5,000 a year on the card before you are eligible to get frequent flier mileage credit.

- *Diner's Club* card holders are credited with ½ mile per dollar charged and there's a choice of eight participating airlines. No extra fees or annual minimums.

If you decide to use a card that gives you frequent flier mileage, you have a good reason not to use other cards. Nearly all department stores now accept major credit cards, so stop using store cards. Does your supermarket also accept credit cards? If there is no discount for cash purchases, you can add on a lot of frequent-flier miles there.

▶ USE A DISCOVER CARD

Marlin Mullins of Hammond, Louisiana, wrote to tell us about his credit-card strategy, a good one. He uses a Discover card (no annual fee; 800-347-2683), which gives him annual cash rebates that range from .025 percent on charges up to $1,000 to 1 percent on charges exceeding $3,000. He pays the full balance owed on the card each month using a check from an interest-bearing checking account. He figures that on purchases made at the beginning of the credit-card billing cycle, before he makes his payment he has had 45 days' free use of the item as well as 45 days of interest on the money—plus a year-end bonus when he is credited with rebates earned.

A 1 percent cash rebate is preferable to frequent-flier mileage credits if you don't intend to fly anyplace. If you do, though, a frequent-flier mile for every dollar you spend is worth more than a 1 percent rebate. The other problem we see is that the Discover card is not as widely accepted as Visa or MasterCard.

▶ THE BEST SOURCE OF A LOAN

As a general rule, the worst possible source of a loan is the seller of the product. See Chapter 5 for a discussion of dealer automobile loans, the most common of many loans made by sellers who actually get a kickback (which you pay for) from the ultimate source of the money. Even if the seller is self-financing the loan, you can bet that you'll be paying a far higher rate than you would had you borrowed from a bank.

Finance companies deal with the most unsophisticated borrowers, which is how they get away with borrowing money themselves and then relending it at a much higher rate.

The best source of a loan? Your own resources. If you've got $20,000 in a money market fund, and need to buy a new car, take it out of the fund and pay cash. You'll still have some emergency funds left over (you have no business buying a car for more than $15,000 if all you've got saved is $20,000), and no money market fund is paying you as much in interest as you'll pay to a lender.

With that lecture over, a few other alternatives, none as good:

If you have a cash-value insurance policy, check out a loan from your insurance company. If you are fortunate enough to be a member of an active credit union, you will probably be able to get a low-cost loan there. You may also be able to borrow money from your profit-sharing fund where you work; check with your benefits or personnel department. After that, banks are still your best choice. See the next few tips for what to look for and what to avoid.

▶ A ROSE IS A ROSE IS A ROSE, BUT A LENDER'S INTEREST RATE ISN'T

Your bank agrees to lend you $10,000 at 10 percent for one year. How much will you pay in interest?

The obvious answer is 10 percent of $10,000, or $1,000. The actual answer will almost certainly be different, and higher. Unfortunately, the interest rates quoted by lenders don't tell the whole story. The next few tips do.

▶ SIMPLE-INTEREST/SINGLE-PAYMENT LOANS

This is the least expensive way to borrow money. You pay interest only on the money you still owe. Using a single-payment method, you would take the $10,000 and at the end of the year make one payment to the lender of $11,000. You have had the use of the full $10,000 for the entire twelve months and have paid $1,000—10 percent—in interest.

Alternatively, if you pay off a 10 percent simple-interest loan in twelve monthly installments, your total interest payments will be only $550. Why? Because you will not have had the use of $10,000 for the full twelve months. Your first monthly payment of $879 would include interest charges of $83 and a partial payment of $796 on the principal. Your second monthly payment of $879 would consist of a smaller interest payment and a larger partial payment on the principal because you would now have the use of only $9,204 ($10,000 minus $796) of the principal. And so on, for each of the next eleven months. As the amount of the principal still outstanding diminishes, so does the interest payment.

Either kind of simple-interest loan is highly desirable, but don't count on getting one from any lender unless you are a highly preferred or corporate customer.

▶ DISCOUNTED INTEREST LOANS

Still using our example of a $10,000 one-year loan at 10 percent, with this type of loan the lender deducts the 10 percent interest up front and therefore lends you only $9,000. At the end of the year, you will pay back $10,000 in a single payment.

Not so bad? Let's calculate your true interest rate. You have really borrowed only $9,000 and paid $1,000 in interest. When calculated ($1,000 divided by $9,000), this comes to a true interest rate of 11.11 percent.

It gets much worse. If you take the $9,000 and agree to make twelve monthly payments of $833.30 ($10,000 divided by 12), your effective annual interest rate on the money you have actually had use of comes to almost 20 percent!

You are beginning to understand some of the mysteries of banking. Read on.

▶ ADD-ON INTEREST LOANS

You may also be offered this method by a lender. The $1,000 interest on your $10,000 loan is added on to the principal in the beginning. Then you repay $11,000 in twelve monthly installments. True annual interest: almost 18 percent.

If you are quoted either an "add-on" or "discounted" interest rate, then the true annual interest you will pay will be almost *double* the percentage quoted.

▶ KNOW THE APR—AND MORE

Lenders can and still will quote you an add-on or discounted interest rate, but for the past fifteen years they have also been legally required to tell you the true annual percentage rate (the APR). Unfortunately, too many people still commit to overly expensive loans because the APR isn't mentioned until all the papers are about to be signed. Do not ever commit to a loan until you have seen, in writing, the federally required APR interest on it.

Even then, especially in the case of a complicated loan such as a mortgage, the APR quoted may not take into account some of the expenses you have to incur to get the loan (title insurance fees, credit report fees, application fees, etc.). It gets very complicated indeed, but if you are repaying a loan over a thirty-year period, a difference of ½ percent on a principal of $100,000 can amount to thousands of dollars. If you aren't comfortable doing it yourself, have a good accountant review the figures to arrive at your true loan costs.

▶ SECURED VERSUS UNSECURED LOANS

A secured loan means that you have given the bank some form of collateral as security. If you don't pay the money back, they get to keep the collateral. Your home mortgage is a secured loan, but you can also use stocks, bonds, a car, or any other hard asset as collateral.

An unsecured loan means the bank has extended credit

to you without collateral. When you get an approved line of credit up to a certain amount at your bank and write checks against it, you are in effect taking out an unsecured loan. Banks are careful about the credit ratings of people approved for unsecured loans, but even so you will pay a higher interest rate than if the loan were secured by collateral. You've got to pay it back anyway, so why not secure the loan?

▶ BEWARE THE FLOATING RATE

Banks and other credit institutions love to shift risk from themselves to you. That's why you may be offered a "floating rate" loan, usually tied to the "prime rate" charged by banks to their best corporate customers. You might be offered a loan at "prime plus 3," for instance, meaning your interest payments would always be 3 percent over the current prime rate.

The danger here is the same as it is with an adjustable rate mortgage. Avoid it if at all possible.

▶ THE PENNY PINCHER'S BANK LOAN

Despite the previous example of simple interest/single-payment loans, you should know one thing about them: Banks rarely if ever offer simple-interest/single-payment loans to retail customers. Installment loans of any kind are more profitable. But you can at least try to negotiate. Here's how:

Dealing (ideally) with a bank officer you already know (your branch manager, perhaps), don't say anything about the single-payment method until after you have the bank's agreement on the amount and term of the loan as well as the APR. The bank, of course, will be planning to charge you monthly installments with a fixed monthly payment in which interest payments will gradually decline and payments to principal will gradually increase.

Once you have the commitment, tell your banker you will be willing to pay off the loan in monthly payments over the term agreed upon, and at the APR the bank has quoted. But you want the loan structured as a single-payment loan that allows monthly payments. In other words, you will pay the same amount each month toward the principal, as well as interest at the agreed-upon APR on the principal outstanding.

The result will be that you will pay more than you would under the usual installment method at the beginning of the loan, and less at the end. More important, you will pay less in interest over the term of the loan.

Your banker won't be thrilled with your suggestion, but you'll have a good argument: She has agreed to amount, to term, and to APR, and there's no additional risk to the bank. Why not do it your way?

▶ AVOID AUTO DEALER LOANS

When you take out an auto loan, the car becomes collateral against your monthly payments. Although the car declines in value over the term of the loan, so does the amount of principal you owe. So auto loans are quite safe for lenders to make, even to someone whose credit rating isn't perfect.

Auto loans are also very profitable for dealers. That's because dealers usually have relationships with banks or other big lenders to whom they will sell your loan once they have arranged it. Put in the simplest terms, when you arrange a loan through a dealer, you are paying extra to work with a middleman. Go to the ultimate lender yourself and save money.

▶ PAYING OFF EARLY: BEWARE THE RULE OF 78s

Although illegal in some states, the majority of them still allow lenders to use an accounting method called "the rule of 78s" when a loan is paid off early. If you decide to prepay a loan that uses this method—even if there is no prepayment penalty in your loan agreement—you will end up paying a much higher interest rate than the agreement calls for. Here's how it works in a loan with a one-year term:

The first month, you would pay 12/78 of the interest,

the second month 11/78, the third 10/78, and so on down to 1/78 in the final month. If you pay the loan off at the end of the sixth month, and the lender activates the rule of 78s, you will have already paid 57/78 (12+11+10+9+8+7) in interest—not half the amount owed, but nearly three-quarters of the total.

When you read a loan agreement, look carefully for references to prepayment penalties, the rule of 78s, or the term "the sum of the digits." What you want instead is a simple interest loan or an agreement that uses the actuarial method for computing interest due on prepayments. *Ask for it.*

▶ NO INTEREST CHARGES! BUY NOW! 24 MONTHS TO PAY!

And maybe you believe in the tooth fairy. The interest charges are hidden in the bloated price of the car or whatever else you are buying. It is still an installment loan, and the dealer can still sell it to a bank for a profit. In practice, because such offers are particularly attractive to unsophisticated borrowers and no APR need be declared, what you end up paying is higher than what you would have paid by buying the car for an honest price and paying interest on the loan.

Making Money with Your Money

Penny-pinching is easier when you have extra dollars to pinch. This chapter will suggest a few ways to make the money you earn work harder to make you more money.

The word "tip" has a deservedly negative reputation when it comes to investment advice. But unlike the tips your brother-in-law gives you about hot stocks, ours concentrate on the decisions you must make among saving and investing methods and techniques. (Tip #1: Avoid hot stock tips.) Or they suggest cheaper ways to make different kinds of investments.

As a brief checklist, they are useful. For complete investment advice, go elsewhere. Where? That's not an easy question, so we'll start with a couple of basic rules.

▶ DON'T BLINDLY TRUST EXPERTS

Yes, you can hire a financial planner to take complete charge of every aspect of your life that involves money— your household budget, savings plans, investments, and retirement. You can take your allowance like a teenager and not worry about a thing. Naturally you will have less money to manage, since the fees for this kind of all-encompassing financial planning don't come cheap. And what happens if you choose an adviser who is inept, unlucky, or even dishonest?

Year after year, there are news stories about rich and famous athletes and show business personalities who lose millions or are even bankrupted because they trusted an adviser to make all their financial decisions. The media seldom report on the millions of middle-class people who rely on other people and end up paying big fees for terrible results.

The first and most important tip about saving and investing is to learn enough about the subject so that you can trust the one person who is ultimately responsible: yourself. You don't have to become an expert, but you have to know enough to decide what you want to hire experts for, how to choose good ones, and when it is just as easy—and cheaper—to do it yourself.

▶ GET INTERESTED IN YOUR MONEY

That's different than getting interest *on* your money. If you have enough penny-pinching instincts to save hundreds of dollars a year by shopping wisely and saving on energy bills, you can't afford to skip the financial pages of your newspaper. What's happening to interest rates, federal budget deficits, the value of the dollar, and the economy has a direct bearing on your money and your future.

To get comfortable with the idea of being responsible for your money, first read the tips in this chapter. Frankly, if you have no background at all in money management, you're likely to be a bit confused, even though the tips may help you with specific questions or problems. So turn next to a book on basic investing principles. Among the good ones at your library, Andrew Tobias's *The Only Other Investment Guide You'll Ever Need* is sensible, quite comprehensive, and more fun to read than most.

After you've read one or two books, begin spending a couple of hours a week reading newspapers (nothing beats *The Wall Street Journal*) and magazines (*Money* and *Kiplinger's Personal Finance Magazine* are fine, but working your way up to *Forbes* and *Barron's* is a reasonable goal).

Keeping up with a rapidly changing world and new investment possibilities is essential. The days of putting your money in "safe" investments and never worrying about them are over.

▶ GET FREE FINANCIAL ADVICE

No bank, brokerage firm, insurance company, or mutual fund manager will give away a free booklet unless they think you may become a customer after you read it. But that self-interest doesn't mean the information provided is worthless. The opposite is often the case. Calling an 800 number is free, and you'll find all kinds of useful, informative booklets offered at the bottom of ads placed by different financial institutions. The only cost to you will be the time spent answering a few subsequent telephone calls soliciting your business.

One especially noteworthy example is a first-rate guide to financial planning for retirement offered free by T. Rowe Price (800-638-5660). T. Rowe Price mutual funds are suggested, naturally, but only after all the major financial issues are confronted and you have been led through a series of personalized worksheets that help you decide exactly what you will need and how much you will have available.

All twelve Federal Reserve Banks publish free monthly newsletters on economic conditions and financial matters. Simply write to any (or all, if you want them) Federal Reserve Bank and ask to be put on their mailing list. There are Federal Reserve Banks in Atlanta, Boston, Chicago, Cleveland, Dallas, Kansas City, Minneapolis, New York, Philadelphia, Richmond, and St. Louis.

▶ PROTECT YOURSELF BEFORE INVESTING

Unless you are single with no dependents, life insurance coverage is a priority before any investment activity. So are the other kinds of insurance (see Chapter 3) that protect you against the risks of serious financial loss. And you should have enough readily available cash in a bank or mutual fund or money market fund to cover three months of your living expenses—in case of sudden illness, loss of a job, or a temporary disability. When these bases are covered, you are ready to develop an investment plan.

▶ PAY OFF HIGH-INTEREST DEBTS

It is silly to keep $2,000 in a money market account paying 4 percent taxable interest at the same time you owe $2,000 on your bank credit card and are paying 17 percent in non-tax-deductible interest. The first way to get more income from your income is to pay off any high-interest debt—normally everything but your home mortgage and home equity loans, which are tax-deductible.

▶ OWN A HOME

Is this an investment strategy? And if so, is it still a good one? For decades, as residential real estate prices in most parts of the country rose every year, it was virtually an article of faith among personal financial advisers that owning a home was the single best investment anyone could make. Then the end of the boom came. In some areas, houses have declined in value by 30 percent or more in one year. A lot of people now question the old conventional wisdom.

It is possible they are right. But there have been other periods of depressed real estate prices in American history. In the long run, prices have rebounded. In the long run, the odds are still high that the value of your home will at least keep pace with inflation.

"In the long run" doesn't help much if you buy at a market high and are forced to sell in a depressed market a couple of years later. If you don't plan on staying in your area for a minimum of five years, renting might be safer. Otherwise, home ownership is still a sound investment. You have to live somewhere, and paying rent is a certain way not to build any equity. The one major tax shelter left to most people is the deduction of mortgage interest payments on their federal income tax returns. There would probably be a full-scale middle class revolution if the politicians ever tried to change that.

Finally, if the real estate market still hasn't recovered as you are reading this, if the gloom and doomsday predictions are shared by just about everybody, you just may have the buying opportunity of a lifetime. Historically, the best buying opportunities come when there are more eager sellers than buyers. Just as the best time to sell is usually when everyone else is jumping on the bandwagon to buy.

▶ TAKE ADVANTAGE OF TAX-DEFERRED INVESTMENT PLANS

You have certain investment goals—money for a child's college education, a new house, a wedding, redecorating, etc.—that probably can't be achieved with tax-deferred investments. That's because the government assesses a big penalty if you withdraw money from a tax-deferred plan before you are fifty-nine and a half.

When your investment goal is a comfortable retirement, though, your first and best decision is to take maximum advantage of tax-deferred investment opportunities. "Tax-deferred" means that no taxes are collected on the money you make until you withdraw it. By avoiding annual taxes for many years, a lot more of your money stays invested, earning interest and appreciating in value.

If your employer has a salary deduction plan, put every dollar possible into it. Many companies match whatever you put in with a contribution of their own to your account—typically 50 percent. This is the best deal possible. Grab it.

Any personal finance guide will explain the ins and outs of IRAs, Keogh plans, 401(k) and 403(b) plans, and SEPs (Simplified Employee Pension plans, which allow employers to contribute to employees' individual IRAs). These are all tax-advantaged ways to invest, and you should understand how each works.

▶ NEVER BET IT ALL ON ONE SCENARIO

No one can predict the future. Not your brother-in-law with a hot tip about a stock that can't miss, not the chairman of the Federal Reserve Bank, not the most successful money managers in the world. Trust no one who is absolutely certain about what will happen to the stock market in the next few months, or where interest rates will be next year. *No one knows.*

In the long run (yes, again), although they may invest huge sums based on a certain future scenario, most money managers who stay in business always diversify their assets in some form or another. They may think the economy will boom and the stock market will go up 500 points in the next year, but they don't bet everything on that one outcome.

Most of us should diversify our investments in two ways. First, we should own different categories of assets: real estate (usually just our homes), equities (stocks and mutual stock funds), fixed-income investments (bonds and certificates of deposit), and cash equivalents (money market funds and savings accounts).

As a general rule, the younger you are the more heavily weighted your long-term investments should be in equities and real estate. That's because, historically, over a long period of time those investments have produced a greater return than bonds. If you are five years away from retirement, you will want to become more conservative, shifting some assets into investments that will pay you a fixed income and protecting yourself from the possibility of a long slump in the stock market. Even then, as a hedge against future inflation, you should own some equities or some real estate that may appreciate in value as well as produce income.

The second way you should diversify is within asset categories. Don't invest all of your equity money in one stock or buy the bonds of just one company. In fact, don't even invest in just one kind of stock or bond—the oil industry, for example, or computers or airlines. You will reduce your risks considerably by owning a portfolio that isn't completely dependent on one future scenario coming true.

If you have $100,000 or more to invest and can establish a good relationship with a knowledgeable broker, you can diversify by investing in individual stocks and bonds. Otherwise, except for investments in U.S. Treasuries (see below), your best alternative is to invest in mutual funds. The different types of funds give you a way to diversify categories (stocks or bonds) as well as to own widely diversified portfolios within those categories.

▶ HOW TO CHOOSE A MUTUAL FUND

Since 400-page books are written on this topic and we cover the subject in about that many words, don't expect much detail in what follows. But there is an easy, three-step way to narrow your choices down from thousands of funds to a few that will meet your objectives.

(1) Exactly what are you looking for in a fund? Growth? Income? What kind of risk are you willing to take? Do you want a fund that invests all or part of your money outside the United States? Only you can decide what investment philosophy and strategies suit you best, although some of those 400-page books may help you clarify them. There is no one mutual fund that is right for everyone, and if your portfolio is large enough, you should probably diversify into funds with somewhat different objectives and/or investing techniques.

When you feel comfortable with your objectives, it is time to go to the library. Take a look at the annual and/or quarterly mutual fund issues of *Money, Barron's, Kiplinger's Personal Finance Magazine, Business Week,* and *Forbes.* Each uses somewhat different criteria in examining and ranking funds, but all include data about past performance, investment objectives, and 800 numbers to call for

Why Dollar-Cost Averaging Works

You've decided that all the arguments about investing in stocks for long-term results make sense. But you've also heard horror stories about buying shares in a mutual fund for $10.00 and seeing them sink to $8.00 in less than a week's time. How do you guard against that?

You don't, because you can't. The stock market averages are always going up or down, and a long bear market (when stock prices fall nearly continuously for months at a time) is no fun for anyone. The fact is, though, that the biggest gains made in stock investments are usually those made by buying in the depths of a bear market when hardly anyone wants to own stocks.

The best investment technique available to people who are putting their money in the stock market for the long term (at least seven to ten years, preferably longer) is dollar-cost averaging. You invest a fixed amount of money each month (or each quarter) in a particular mutual fund. You keep doing this year after year, on exactly the same dates, whether the experts are predicting eternal prosperity or an imminent doomsday. By investing *the same amount each time* you will buy more shares of the fund when prices are low and fewer shares when prices are high.

It's that simple, but it works. Here's an example, exaggerating the price movement of the fund's shares in just one year's time to illustrate the effects of dollar-cost averaging (realistically, it takes a lot longer than this for such a dramatic effect to be apparent):

WITH DOLLAR-COST AVERAGING

Date of purchase	Price per share	Number of shares purchased	Amount invested
Dec 31	$ 6	150	$ 900
Mar 30	$ 3	300	$ 900
Jun 30	$ 9	100	$ 900
Sep 30	$15	60	$ 900
Dec 31	$12	75	$ 900
Totals		685	$4,500

WITHOUT DOLLAR-COST AVERAGING

Price per share	Number of shares purchased	Amount invested
$ 6	100	$ 600
$ 3	100	$ 300
$ 9	100	$ 900
$15	100	$1,500
$12	100	$1,200
	500	$4,500

The same $4,500 invested with dollar-cost averaging gives you 185 more shares than you would have gotten by purchasing a fixed number of shares on the same dates. No matter what the price of the stock is, you own more of it than you would have without dollar-cost averaging.

prospectuses. By this point, you will be able to concentrate on the funds whose objectives match your own.

(2) Now narrow your choices to "no-load" or very "low-load" funds. All the magazines above tell you which funds are no-load. A no-load fund charges no commission on the up-front sale and no fee for the back-end redemption. There have been countless studies of the performance of no-load funds versus load funds, which can charge up to an 8.5 percent commission. None of them have yet made a compelling case that there's any difference in how the funds perform. There are many load funds with superior long-term records, but there are no-load funds that have performed just as well. An initial investment of $1,000 instead of $915 ($1,000 minus an 8.5 percent commission) gives you a head start.

(3) Finally, choose no-load funds with low administrative fees. All you have to do is check *Money* magazine's annual mutual fund issue (February) for a projection of expenses for the leading 1,000 or so funds. If your choice is between a fund with a terrible record whose expenses are projected by *Money* at $50.00 per thousand and another with a superior record with projected expenses of $100, you might want to pay the higher expenses. But higher expenses don't guarantee better results, so if everything else is equal, why not opt for the savings?

By this point you will find your choices narrowed down to a very few funds. Get their prospectuses and read them. Remember that superior past performance is not a guarantee for the future. In fact, we suggest you stay away from the hottest funds of the previous year—the ones ranked at the very top for one-year performance. So much money is flowing into them that their managers may have a hard time investing it as wisely as they did in the past. Find a fund with a good long-term record over five or ten years, take the plunge, and monitor performance against the competition from then on.

▶ BUY MUTUAL FUNDS USING DOLLAR-COST AVERAGING

No matter what else is happening in the world, you will always be able to find one expert predicting that stock prices will double in the next year and another one predicting the opposite. Nor can you rely on consensus opinions; historically, when a vast majority of experts have agreed it was time to buy, it was usually a good time to sell. And vice versa. Except, of course, that once this became known, everyone became a "contrarian" investor and all bets were off about what majority opinions actually meant.

Confusing? Of course. That's what makes a market a market. At any given time, one party to a transaction is convinced it is a good idea to sell at a certain price and another party is equally sure it is a good idea to buy at the same price. There are thousands of professionals who make a living trying to "time" the market, selling and buying at just the right times. Yet over the long term, very few market timers manage to beat the stock market averages.

You simply can't be certain you'll always buy at the best possible time. So many people believe the best strategy is not to worry about timing at all. They use dollar-cost averaging, an especially effective technique if you are investing for long-term results. The example on pages 174 and 175 shows you why.

▶ BUY U.S. TREASURIES DIRECT

You don't have any choice when you want to buy stock in a company. You either pay a brokerage commission or you pay a mutual fund its annual fees as well as any up-front or back-end redemption fees it charges.

But why pay a broker—even a discount broker—as much as $30.00 to $90.00 each time you invest in super-safe U.S. Treasury bills, notes, or bonds? Unless you think you will want to sell the note before it matures, it is actually easier, more convenient, and completely free (except for the price of a stamp) to deal directly with the seller of the bonds—the U.S. Government. Write to the Bureau of Public Debt, Washington, D.C. 20239, or look in the phone book for the number of any Federal Reserve Bank or branch (there are thirty-five of them nationwide). Ask for an application to set up a Treasury Direct account. All you need is your social security number and a bank account where you want your future interest payments and principal deposited. From then on, using the very brief and easily understood forms provided, you can buy any denomination of new Treasury offerings by mail—at exactly the same price a broker would pay.

▶ CHECK OUT OLD U.S. SAVINGS BONDS

Do you still have that $25.00 Series E U.S. Savings Bond Grandpa gave you for your birthday back in 1950 or 1960? If you do, you probably keep it in a safe-deposit box, glance at it once a year, and take for granted that it is still earning interest.

Holders of more than $1.7 billion of old savings bonds are presently making that mistake. Their bonds are no longer earning any interest at all. If you own a bond issued thirty or more years ago, take it to your bank and ask them to check on what it is worth today and if it is still earning interest.

If it isn't, you can exchange an old Series E or EE bond for a Series H bond and delay the tax consequences of redeeming the old bond now. If it is, make sure you note when it will stop earning interest and keep that information in a safe place.

The other mistake many holders of savings bonds make is not knowing that when they redeem their bonds can make quite a difference. That's because interest on savings bonds (after rising monthly for the first two and a half years on new Series E bonds) is calculated only two times a year, and those two times depend on when the bond was issued. The practical effect of this is that if you cash in a bond a week before a calculation date, you lose half a year's interest.

If your bank can't answer your questions about calculation dates on bonds you own, try calling a Federal Reserve Bank. If that doesn't work, call *Savings Bond Informer, Inc.* (313-843-1910). For a small fee, this company will give you calculation dates, redemption values, and current interest rates on any savings bonds you own.

▶ USE DIVIDEND REINVESTMENT PLANS

If you own stocks directly, not through mutual funds, look into automatic dividend reinvestment plans. Many of the largest corporations allow you to invest your dividends in additional shares without paying any service or brokerage fees. This is a painless as well as cost-free way to save and invest.

▶ COMPARE TAX-EXEMPT ALTERNATIVES

The interest on municipal bonds (bonds issued by states, cities, school boards, and other local and state authorities) are generally not subject to federal income taxation. If you live in the state in which they are issued, you also won't have to pay state income taxes on the interest. This can make municipal bonds and mutual funds that invest in them an attractive alternative to other fixed-income investments, especially if you live in a state with high income taxes.

The mistake many people make is to avoid taxes just for the sake of avoiding them. What you are interested in is the after-tax return, and there is a quick way to compare the after-tax return of a tax-exempt bond or fund.

Suppose you are in a 28 percent federal and 8 percent state tax bracket. Here's how you would analyze a yield of 6½ percent that was tax-exempt in your state:

(1) Because state taxes are exempt from federal taxes, calculate your "effective" state tax. To do that, multiply 8 percent by 72 percent (100 percent minus your federal tax rate of 28 percent). That calculation is $.08 \times .72 = .057$.

(2) Add your "effective" state tax rate to your federal tax rate. That calculation is 28 percent + 5.7 percent = 33.7 percent.

(3) Subtract 33.7 percent from 100 percent to get 66.3 percent.

(4) Divide the after-tax yield of 6½ percent by 66.3 percent (.065 ÷ .663) to get 9.8 percent.

All other things being equal, only if you can get a taxable yield of more than 9.8 percent are you better off than with the 6½ percent tax-free yield.

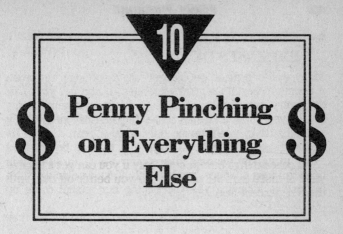

10

$ Penny Pinching on Everything Else $

Here is a final grab bag of tips that didn't seem to fit under any of the previous chapter headings—in no particular order, and covering drugs, cosmetics, college expenses, pets, kids, movies, lawn mowers . . .

▶ DON'T TRUST ANYBODY'S BILLS

Keep good enough records of credit card and charge purchases to be able to check monthly bills for errors. Computers don't often make mistakes, but the people who punch in the numbers do.

One recent study of supermarkets using scanners at their checkout counters estimated that over 40 percent of customer bills contained some kind of error. The main cause of this was that price changes—including items on sale—had not been entered so the scanner could identify them. Check every supermarket tape.

▶ STRETCH REGULAR EXPENSES OUT

Many well-organized people get into a spending rut when it comes to certain regular expenses. If you get your hair cut every two weeks at $12.00 an appointment, that's $312 a year. If you stretch those fourteen-day intervals by just four days, you'll spend only $240 a year. One of us wears disposable contact lenses that have to be changed every week. By wearing glasses for two or three days in between lens changes, we use only forty weeks' worth of disposable lenses a year—reducing our annual costs by nearly 25 percent.

Reexamine every expense you make regularly. You may be surprised at how easy it is to cut back by stretching out.

▶ BUY HALF SHARES WITH OTHER PENNY PINCHERS

You use your lawn mower once a week and get it serviced once a year. If you buy your next one cooperatively with your next-door neighbor, it will probably last just as long, you'll still service it just once a year, and only one of you will be stuck with storing it. Most important, you'll cut your costs by 50 percent.

There are a number of things you need but don't use very often that can be bought cooperatively with trustworthy friends or neighbors. Garden tools are the most obvious examples, but sewing machines, magazine subscriptions, indoor power tools, and many other items are possibilities to consider.

▶ BARTER SERVICES WITH NEIGHBORS

A retired friend is an avid gardener with too small a yard to keep him happy. His neighbor, who always hated any kind of gardening, now gets complete, loving care of his grounds—free. In return, he buys all the garden supplies for both houses and prepares the gardener's annual tax forms.

▶ TRY BARTER OPTIONS ELSEWHERE

If you like the idea of bartering, you don't have to limit it to neighbors. It's anybody's guess how many accountants regularly barter free tax services with dentists for free dental work, or how many garage owners barter automobile maintenance for carpentry work on their houses. Hundreds of millions of barter transactions take place in the United States every year between people who trade goods and/or services with no exchange of money. Especially if you have a special skill, barter is something to consider whenever you are buying goods or services from an owner/manager or a professional. *Caveat:* IRS regulations make most barter transactions taxable.

▶ WAIT THREE MONTHS FOR MOVIES

Except for the biggest hits, most new movies are now available on video within three to five months. Renting a movie for $3.00 instead of paying $12.00 for tickets for two makes sense, unless there are special production values lost on the small home screen. Just as sensible: Borrow videos, particularly classic films, from your library, which also usually has records, cassettes, and CDs.

▶ FACE THE TRUTH ABOUT COSMETICS? NOT LIKELY

Deep down, you know the cosmetics makers sell hope, dreams, and fantasies. You know the ingredients in a $100 bottle of perfume may cost less than the $3.00 price of the bottle the perfume comes in. You know that nothing that comes in a box is really going to make you instantly beautiful, desirable, or younger.

So what? Life is not a matter of penny pinching alone. But even if you don't give up that expensive fragrance or switch to a cheaper brand of lipstick, perhaps you might consider the few money-saving tips that follow.

▶ DEEP-CONDITION YOUR HAIR FOR PENNIES

You can spend a lot of dollars on expensively packaged potions, but none will do a better job than this:

Beat together one egg and equal amounts—about one-third cup—of water and olive oil. Work the mixture into dry hair, leave on for one hour, then rinse thoroughly before shampooing and conditioning hair as usual.

▶ SAVE ON SKIN MOISTURIZERS

There is nothing a $20.00 skin moisturizer can do for you that won't be accomplished just as well by a $3.00 product. Or a 49-cent one—Vaseline Petroleum Jelly.

It *is* likely you may find the oil in some other moisturizer more pleasant. But all moisturizers contain some kind of oil, even those that claim to be oil-free; they are simply defining "oil" differently. The only thing that really moisturizes your skin is water, best applied through proper humidity in your house, by cutting back on hot water (which dehydrates the skin) in baths and showers, and by just splashing it on. All any moisturizer does is help hold water on your skin, and the only ingredient in any of them that does that is some form of oil.

If you want to use Vaseline, don't towel dry after a bath or shower. Wait a minute or two and, while still damp, apply the Vaseline. Too messy? At least switch to something inexpensive that has a fragrance you like. And don't bother with different mixtures for hands, feet, elbow, neck, etc. They are interchangeable, but avoid using too oily a product on your face.

▶ SAVE ON ASTRINGENTS AND TONERS

The problem with penny-pinching advice about cosmetics is that nobody wants to hear it. The beautiful packages and ads insist that the $20.00 8-ounce bottles of astringents or toners, used to clean and tighten pores after washing your face, perform some kind of magic.

Witch hazel ($1.99 a quart at drugstores) feels good, has no unpleasant odor, and works every bit as well. Some

things haven't improved since your great-grandmother's
time.

▶ GET FREE SAMPLES AT THE
COSMETICS COUNTER

They are seldom offered, but when you buy something at
a department store cosmetics counter ask about free
samples. The more you buy, the more generous the
saleswoman will be.

Don't forget the ubiquitous "gift with purchase" offers
either. Even if you refuse to give up those $20.00 moistur-
izers, at least you can get something free with them.

▶ BUY COSMETICS BY MAIL

Beautiful Visions (810 Broadway, Hicksville, NY 11801;
516-576-9000) sells brand name cosmetics and toiletries
at very substantial discounts (up to 90 percent on some
famous-name perfumes that probably aren't selling too
well elsewhere). The catalog is free.

▶ THINK GENERIC IN THE
DOCTOR'S OFFICE

Too many busy doctors still automatically use a brand
name when writing a prescription. When you see your
doctor pick up a pen to write your prescription, quickly
ask if he or she will write it generically. Nine times out of
ten, there's no reason at all not to save the money.

Also, don't be shy about asking your doctor if he or she
has any free samples of the drug being prescribed, especially if it is for very short-term use. The drug companies
flood doctors' offices with samples and many doctors are
happy to get rid of them.

▶ JOIN THE AARP

Probably a majority of people celebrating (well, *observing*)
a fiftieth birthday get what some younger friend thinks of
as a great joke gift—a $5.00 membership in the American
Association of Retired Persons. The joke, of course, turns

out to be that most eligible fifty-year-olds soon discover that membership in the AARP (202-434-2777 for information) is one of the great penny-pinching bargains of the century.

In addition to a quite readable bimonthly magazine, membership entitles you to 10 to 15 percent discounts at many hotels and car rentals (and higher discounts at a few others), excursion rates on some airlines that are 10 percent less than their cheapest published rates, and the opportunity to buy prescription and nonprescription drugs from the AARP's very efficient and very cheap discount mail-order pharmacy.

▶ BUY PRESCRIPTION DRUGS BY MAIL

If you are too young to join the AARP, there are other discount mail-order pharmacies whose prices you should check out, especially if you must take some medication over a long period of time. (Obviously, if your doctor prescribes an antibiotic, you can't wait ten days to have it delivered.) Because these companies buy in bulk quantities and have low overhead, they can usually offer prices on both brand name and generic drugs that are even lower than those of discount drugstores. All of the companies listed here also sell over-the-counter medications such as aspirin, sun blocks, and cold remedies at low discount prices. They will quote prices by mail and also send you catalogs. *Pharmail* (800-237-8927); *Action-Mail Order* (800-452-1976); *Medi-Mall* (800-331-1458)

▶ BUY READING GLASSES, SUNGLASSES, OR CONTACT LENSES BY MAIL

There are mail-order services offering prescription eyeglasses (see *The Wholesale-By-Mail Catalog*, described on page 72), but we prefer the convenience of trying on different frames at nearby discount optical stores. Reading glasses, sunglasses, and contacts are a different matter.

If you need simple magnification, nonprescription reading glasses are available in our area either in discount drug-stores, where we've never been able to find an acceptable style, or in optical stores, where even the "discount" prices seem inordinately high.

- *Precision Optical* (for a $1.00 catalog, write Dept. J6, Rochelle, IL 61068; or call 815-562-2174) offers a very good mail order alternative. In addition to half frames, clear bifocals, and other magnifiers, they sell sunglasses and other nonprescription optical devices at very reasonable prices.
- *Sunglasses USA* (800-872-7297) has a free catalog offering big discounts on Bausch & Lomb, Ray-Ban, and other brand name sunglasses.
- *Dial a Contact Lens* (800-872-7297) and *Lens Direct* (800-772-5367) will both give you quick discounted price quotes on any contact lens prescription. Prices may vary; check both before ordering.

▶ GET PETS FREE

It is possible you will find a purebred cat or dog at an animal shelter. More likely you'll choose from mixed-breed animals. Either way, good shelters give away (sometimes charging a small fee or donation) healthy, vaccinated dogs and cats that are often in better shape than animals sold by pet stores.

▶ MAKE OWNING A PET LESS EXPENSIVE

It is easy to spend $1,000 a year on food, medical care, grooming, and other needs of a dog or cat. It is also easy to cut some of those expenses by ordering pet supplies from one of the national mail-order discounters. Among those that offer savings of from 35 to 75 percent that you can write for free catalogs:

- *The Kennel Vet Company*, Box 835, Bellmore, NY 11710. Nutritionally balanced foods, leashes, health products, kennels, etc. Mainly for dogs, but also stocks cat supplies.
- *The Dog's Outfitter*, Box 2010, Hazleton, PA 18201. As good for cat supplies as for dog's, despite the name.

- *R. C. Steele,* 800-872-3773. Dogs only—big savings and great service.
- *Doctors Foster & Smith,* 800-826-7206. Veterinary products and more, for cats, dogs, horses.

▶ BUY GOLF AND TENNIS EQUIPMENT BY MAIL

Las Vegas Discount Golf & Tennis (5325 South Valley Blvd., Las Vegas, NV 89118; 702-798-6847) sells name brand golf clubs, tennis racquets, and other golf and racquet sports equipment at large discounts. There are stores in a number of states, the catalog is free, and they'll quote prices by phone or by mail with SASE.

▶ JOIN THE Y

Prices vary, and so does what is offered. But in many cities and towns across America, the Ys have wonderful facilities and offer incredible bargains to swimmers, runners, racquet sports players, and fitness enthusiasts.

▶ CALL FOR HOUSEPLANT BARGAINS

Companies that rent houseplants to offices often sell those they can't use at a fraction of their usual retail price. If you are in the market for some new houseplants, check the Yellow Pages (under "plants") and make a few telephone calls.

▶ REDUCE A CHILD'S ASSETS BEFORE FINANCIAL AID FOR COLLEGE

More than 75 percent of students attending college today receive some kind of financial aid, and most of that aid is based on need. Even families with incomes as high as $75,000 a year can get financial assistance, but they have to prove need based on what is called "Congressional Methodology Need Analysis."

When you apply for financial aid, you will fill out a very complicated form that lays bare your income and assets as well as any assets your child has. It is important to know that only 5.6 percent of your assets are considered available for the costs of college, but 35 percent of your child's assets are.

What this means is that you have good reason to reduce any assets your child has *before* you file the financial aid documents. Buy the computer that will be needed in college—as well as clothes, airline tickets, etc.—using his or her assets, not yours.

▶ PLAN WAY AHEAD FOR COLLEGE FINANCIAL AID

The process of applying for and receiving grants and loans for a college education is always time-consuming and usually frustrating. But it is not as mysterious as it seems to those confronting all the forms and choices for the first time. Your library has books that tell you everything you need to know; you might also start by getting a copy of *Parents' Guide to the College Admission Process* ($4.00 from the National Association of College Admissions Counselors, 1631 Prince Street, Alexandria, VA 22313).

Even if your child is years away from college, if you think you will need or want financial aid when the time comes, go to your library now. What you learn may very well affect your saving, investing, and tax strategies for the intervening years.

Here's one specific example: Suppose your child plans to enter college as a freshman in September 1994. The financial aid package he or she will get will depend on what your income was in 1993. That gives you a big incentive to defer income from that year (see Chapter 3).

Also, you want to be ready to file for financial aid as early as possible. Most colleges accept forms as early as January 1; mail yours the day after Christmas. The reason: Many colleges make grants (which you don't have to repay) on a first-come, first-served basis. The later you file, the more likely you'll be getting a higher ratio of loans (which you do have to repay) in your package.

In addition to the books on financial aid at your library, call the Federal Student Aid Information Center at 800-

433-3243 for all the forms you will need as well as advice on how to fill them out.

▶ CASH IN U.S. SAVINGS BONDS TO PAY TUITION

If your adjusted gross income doesn't exceed a set limit (currently $62,500 for joint filers, but adjusted annually for inflation), all the interest you earn on Series EE U.S. Savings Bonds is income-tax free when the bonds are redeemed to pay any part of your child's college tuition bills. The interest on Series EE Bonds changes every six months, and is set to equal 85 percent of the average yield on five-year Treasuries. But if you hold an EE Bond for five years or more, you are guaranteed at least 6 percent interest. Given the 100 percent safety factor combined with the tax-free benefit, that's a very attractive return if interest rates are low.

▶ SHIP COLLEGE-BOUND KIDS OFF EARLY

This is a bit radical, but worth mentioning. Two years ago, the son of friends of ours, then a junior in high school, decided he wanted to go to a state university outside his own state. Tuition fees there were far higher for out-of-state residents. He went to live with an uncle and aunt during his senior year, establishing a new residence, and qualified for the far lower in-state tuition. He's now a freshman and the family will save at least $24,000 over a four-year period.

▶ STOP BUYING LOTTERY TICKETS

If you want to dream about being a multimillionaire, fanta-size instead about an unknown relative dying and leaving his riches to you. It is a likelier scenario than a lottery win. State lotteries are nothing but another form of tax, and unfortunately this tax falls most heavily on those who can least afford it.

Here are some numbers to inspire you: Instead of

throwing away $100 a year on lottery tickets for the next fifty years, invest that money in an aggressive growth mutual fund that averages a 16 percent return a year. At the end of fifty years you will have $1,043,565 instead of a pile of worthless tickets.

▶ GET FREE CONSUMER ADVICE FROM THE GOVERNMENT

We've mentioned a couple of specific booklets available from the Government Printing Office in this book, but there are hundreds of them. Many are free and few cost more than a couple of dollars (unless you take into account the taxes you pay to write, produce, and print millions of copies a year).

One of the most useful is an 8½" × 11" 96-page booklet called *The Consumer's Resource Catalog*. In addition to some reasonable (if not exactly streetwise) advice on how to be a smart consumer, this catalog lists addresses and telephone numbers of whom to write to at different corporations, including car companies, with a complaint. It also gives addresses and telephone numbers of different state and federal agencies, regulators, authorities, and commissions. It is a very handy book to have, and it is free.

The government will give you advice on buying a used car (50 cents), healthy snacking (free), and traveling abroad (free). It will tell you what to do about a common cold (free), asbestos in the home ($1.00), or a child with a speech disorder (50 cents). It has booklets on careers and education, exercise and weight control, federal programs, food and nutrition, health, housing, money management, parenting, small business, travel, and hobbies.

You may not find every answer you want, but at these prices you may at least want to know what's available. You can get a free copy of the catalog that describes all the booklets, *Consumer Information Catalog*, as well as a copy of *Consumer's Resource Handbook* (identify it also as item #586X) by writing: S. James, Consumer Information Center-V, Box 100, Pueblo, CO 81002.

▶ LOOK FOR BARGAINS EVERYWHERE

They exist. No matter what you are buying, there are nearly always alternative sources and quick ways to find them. There are usually ways to negotiate better deals. Strategies that work in one area can often be adapted to work well in others. Use the tips you've read in these pages, but don't stop there.

If you are lucky, one of the things your taxes pay for is a good free library system. Use it. Ask librarians where to find information that will help you make major purchase decisions. Borrow cookbooks, travel guides, how-to references, and books on investing and saving. When you discover you are using a book constantly, go to a bookstore and buy it.

Things change. If you want to make your dollar go as far as possible, you've got to keep up. We know very well that the day after this book goes to press, someone will share with us a terrific new money saving tip that should have been included. We'll keep looking. You should, too.

▶ PINCH PENNIES, NOT KIDS, FRIENDS, OR YOUR SENSE OF HUMOR

Saving money and not wasting any are worthwhile activities, but only if they don't interfere with more important things in your life. Wasting a few dollars is better than jumping on your kids every time they forget to turn out the lights. And saving money should never get in the way of enjoying what you spend it on.

Keep things in perspective. Penny pinching is a rewarding means to an end, not the definition of a complete, well-rounded lifestyle.

Appendix: Starting a Penny-Pincher's Budget

Let's not kid ourselves. If there were a truly quick and easy way to start a workable budget, why would most people spend their lives avoiding it?

On the other hand, once you have made the initial effort and gotten used to the process, you will probably find your budget is not only easy to work with but also makes your life easier in a number of important ways. It may take an extra hour or two a month, but you will always know such things as:

- What progress (or lack of it) you are making toward your most important financial goals
- What categories of spending may be in danger of getting out of hand
- What categories of spending seem excessive to you and which ones you want to cut back
- When it is okay to make a major expenditure, and when it may be dangerous

- Where the money will come from to pay that upcoming insurance premium or to replace the refrigerator that just bit the dust
- When money is coming in, and when it has to go out

Don't start reading the rest of this appendix until you have at least a couple of uninterrupted hours ahead of you. Within that time, you should be able to do much of the work necessary on the worksheets that are needed to start your budget plan. You are also going to need a lot of records from at least the past twelve months, including tax returns, withholding information from your salary checks, credit card statements, check stubs, bank statements, records of medical expenses, and more. Try to assemble as much of that as you can right now.

No, please, don't give up. The process won't be difficult if you follow the step-by-step approach suggested. Don't jump ahead. Things will make a lot more sense if you are completely familiar with one worksheet before moving on to the next one.

FIRST FIGURE OUT WHAT YOU HAVE RIGHT NOW

Before you get into the nitty-gritty of an operating budget, it is a good idea to look at the big picture first. That's what the Net Worth Worksheet on pages 196 and 197 will establish. It may take an hour or so, and maybe a couple of telephone calls to figure out all the numbers. But knowing your net worth is the most meaningful way to keep score in your overall financial plan.

Your net worth is simply the difference between what you own—your assets—and what you owe—your liabilities. It is like a snapshot of your financial health, accurate only at that moment. It will change from day to day, week to week, month to month. There's no reason to calculate it more than once or twice a year, but it is important to do it then. How else will you know what progress you are making?

The best way to calculate your net worth is at about the same time each year. Many people do it when they work on their income taxes before April 15.

What you'll be doing, of course, is comparing each year's worksheet with the last. Keep them all. Ideally, each year the "Net Worth" number at the bottom will increase. If it doesn't, you've got to figure out a way either to make more money or to spend less. A good operating family budget will help you do just that.

Most of the entries necessary in the worksheet are self-explanatory. A few tips and suggestions:

- Be as accurate as you can, but don't worry if you have to make some estimates. Everyone does. The important thing is to use the same criteria each year when you make your estimates. If you are basing your estimate of the current value of your house on what a real estate agent has told you, call the same agent next year. (It is probably a good idea to reduce any agent's estimate by 10 percent; they are notoriously optimistic, especially when estimating the value of a house they may get a chance to list.)

- Use current market values. Your car is worth less than it was last year (check the books in your library). Your life insurance cash values are worth more (call your agent if you aren't sure). You may be certain that your coin collection is going to appreciate rapidly, but be honest: If you had to sell it tomorrow, what would you get?

- If you own your own business, you know there is no precise way to tell what it's worth at any given time unless stock in the company is publicly traded. The best way to approach this problem is to be extremely conservative. Estimate what your interest in the business would be worth if (1) you were no longer able to manage it and (2) your family had to sell it quickly.

- Unless you have some genuine antiques, your home furnishings are not worth a great deal, no matter what you paid for them.

- If you have outstanding loans but can't find how much

Net Worth Worksheet

Date _____

(update at least once a year)

ASSETS:	Current value
Cash on hand	$_____
Checking/savings accounts	_____
Money market funds/CDs	_____
CMA/Credit Union accounts	_____
Life insurance cash values	_____
(A) *Total cash assets*	$_____
Stocks/corporate bonds	$_____
Municipal bonds	_____
Mutual funds	_____
Other	_____
(B) *Total liquid investments*	$_____
Personal residence	$_____
Vacation/second home	_____
Rental property	_____
Real estate partnerships	_____
(C) *Total real estate investments*	$_____
Business interests/partnerships	$_____
Other	_____
(D) *Total other investments*	$_____
IRAs	$_____
Pension accounts	_____
Profit sharing plan accounts	_____
401(k) plan/ESOP assets	_____
Savings, bonus, or thrift plans	_____
Keogh plan assets	_____
Other	_____
(E) *Total retirement assets*	$_____
Cars/boats	$_____
Jewelry and furs	_____

ASSETS:

Art/collectibles/antiques _____
Household furnishings _____
Other _____

   (F) *Total Personal Assets* $_____

TOTAL ASSETS (total A–F) $_____

LIABILITIES: Current amount owed

Credit cards
  Bank $_____
  Store _____
  Other _____
Credit lines
  Overdraft _____
  Home equity lines _____
  Unsecured credit line _____
Income taxes payable _____
Property taxes payable _____

   (G) *Total current liabilities* $_____

Home mortgage $_____
Home equity loan/second mortgage _____
Mortgages on business property _____
Mortgages on investment property _____
Car loans _____
Tuition loans _____
Bank loans _____
Margin loans _____
Life insurance policy loans _____
Other _____

   (H) *Total Long-Term Liabilities* $_____

TOTAL LIABILITIES (total G–H) $_____

NET WORTH (assets minus liabilities) $_____

principal is outstanding, call the lender. Add any prepayment penalties.

■ If you have trouble filling out the worksheet, it is worthwhile getting professional help. But try it on your own, first.

SET GOALS

Have you ever defined and put down on paper your major financial goals? Now is the time to do it. If you are married, this must be done together. Get older kids in on the discussion as well.

Here are a few common goals:

■ Buying a first home or trading up to a better one
■ Getting out of debt
■ Affording children
■ College educations
■ Income for retirement
■ A new car
■ A trip to Europe
■ Money to start a business
■ A new $105,000 Maserati

You don't think many people want a $100,000 car? Of course they do. But after you've listed all of your goals, cross off the ones that are unrealistic. You can still dream about the Maserati; that's what sells lottery tickets.

The next step is to set priorities. Some of your goals are more important than others. Perhaps some can be postponed. If you don't want to do this now, fine. Later on, when you put down a set amount you have to save for long-term goals, you may be forced to set priorities.

Next put down the year in which you want to reach each goal. You might want to be completely out of debt by next year, buy a new car the year after, send four-year-old Jim to college in fourteen years, and retire twenty years after that.

Finally, estimate how much each goal will cost. You don't have to guess how much it may cost years from now; use a dollar figure based on what it would cost if you

Major Goal Worksheet

Date: _____

Goal	Start saving	Need money	Amount	Annual savings needed
(Examples:)				
New car	1/92	1/94	$ 8,000	$4,000
College	1/92	1/06	$40,000	$2,857
(Your goals:)				
TOTAL ANNUAL SAVINGS FOR GOALS				$

bought it today. Yes, inflation will no doubt make long-term goals more expensive, but the money you will be saving and investing to meet your goals will also be growing. Figure on at least staying even with inflation.

Put your goals down in the first column of the Major Goal Worksheet on page 199. In the next column, put down when you plan to start saving for that goal (*now* is the best time). In the third column, put down when you will need the money to make the actual purchase. In the fourth, the dollar amount. In the fifth, divide the dollar amount by the number of years you have to save for this goal. This gives you the annual savings necessary. When you begin your operating budget, divide this by 12 and enter that dollar amount in each month of the Savings for Goals category you'll find in what we call a "Fixed Expenses Worksheet" (pages 204 and 205).

Of course your goals will change, and so will time frames. No problem. Nothing here is engraved in stone. Review and update the Goal Worksheet whenever you like, but certainly do it every time you update your Net Worth.

NOW FIGURE OUT WHAT'S COMING IN

This is usually a lot easier than figuring out where it all goes. Of course you will get a raise this year, but until it happens, don't plan on it. If you are paid on a commission basis, be conservative.

The Income Worksheet that follows asks you to list every item of income you expect during the next year, and to break that down on a monthly basis. Some suggestions:

- In calculating monthly income, remember that not all months will consist of four weekly paychecks. Some months have four checks, others have five. If you get paid weekly, add up thirteen consecutive weeks' checks, then calculate the average check amount by dividing that total by 13. Multiply that average check amount by 4.33, and use that number as your monthly income.
- List only the net amounts of your paychecks (after all deductions for taxes, benefits, etc.).

Income Worksheet

Source	Jan.	Feb.	Mar.	Apr.	May	Jun.	July	Aug.	Sep.	Oct.	Nov.	Dec.	Yearly total
His salary													
Her salary													
Interest													
Dividends													
Bonuses													
Commissions													
Free-lance													
Tax refunds													
Alimony													
Other													
Other													
Other													
MONTHLY TOTALS													

- If you're not sure if a dividend or a bonus will be received in July or August, use the later month.
- Use *minimum* figures when any estimates are necessary (bonuses, free-lance jobs, etc.).
- If you get a raise, revise the worksheet accordingly, but add only the extra take-home pay, not the full amount.
- If your income decreases, revise the worksheet immediately.
- Don't pretend. Don't indulge in wishful thinking. Nobody but you and your spouse will ever see this.

The Income Worksheet starts in January. You can start one in any month, though, as long as you work it out for the next twelve months. Many people have some sources of income that happen on a once-a-year or four-times-a-year basis, so only a full twelve-month period will account for them all on an annual basis.

WHAT MUST GO OUT: FIXED EXPENSES

You may notice that the Fixed Expenses Worksheet that follows makes no provision for food. Yes, you have to eat. But fixed expenses are those you have no control over once you have made certain commitments: your rent or your mortgage, insurance premiums, real estate taxes, etc. If you had to cut back on your monthly food bill, you could do it.

You'll see something else on the Fixed Expenses Worksheet you may want to argue about: saving for goals. Savings? Certainly you can control that amount, can't you?

No. Do you think the utility company is more important than your family's most important goals? Of course not. *Pay yourself first.* That's what your savings represent—a payment to yourself, to your family, to guarantee your futures.

Agreed? Good. Even if you throw out every other piece of advice here, remember the best advice of all: *Pay yourself first.* In the worksheet, divide the amount of your total annual savings for goals by 12, and put that aside each month.

Here are some suggestions for filling out the Fixed Expenses Worksheet:

- To achieve a workable operating budget, you must set aside money for major expenses and savings on a monthly basis, even if a specific expense is incurred annually. If you will pay your semiannual automobile insurance premiums of $600 in March and September, set aside $100 a month, twelve months of the year.

- Nevertheless, you will need a record of when such expenses fall due. That's why you should make *two different copies* of the Fixed Expenses Worksheet—one (A) with full amounts listed in the month in which they are due, the other (B) setting aside monthly amounts as suggested in the paragraph above. The final total of fixed expenses for the year should be the same on each worksheet.

- On fixed expenses that vary month by month, such as telephone and utility bills, add up what you spent in the past twelve months, adjust for new rates you expect or know about, and divide by 12 for Worksheet B. If your utility offers a plan that allows you to pay the same amount each month, you want to use it just to make budgeting easier. If not, and you spent $300 last January and only $50.00 in August, reflect that reality in Worksheet A.

- If you are making installment loan payments or are paying off credit card debt, one of your listed goals should have been to pay them off. List payments by month until you know the debt will be paid off.

- Suggested categories such as medical and dental, drugs and medicine, federal and state taxes ask you to estimate expenses that your company benefits won't pay for or aren't already withheld from your salary. Not easy? You'll be doing a lot of estimating for a while. As you gain experience and revise your budget, you'll get more accurate. See what your records from the past twelve months tell you. Make a monthly estimate.

- Maybe you put down a new washing machine as a goal. If so, you are covered. Many people don't think of a new appliance as a goal, but as an emergency to be

Fixed Expense Worksheet

Must spend/save:	Jan.	Feb.	Mar.	Apr.	May	Jun.	July	Aug.	Sep.	Oct.	Nov.	Dec.	Yearly total
Savings for goals													
Mortgage/rent													
Electric/gas/oil													
Real estate taxes (if not in mortgage payment)													
Home insurance (if not in mortgage payment)													
Water/sewer/ garbage collection													
Home maintenance fund													
Appliance fund													
Federal & state taxes													

Life insurance											
Health/disability insurance											
Medical, dental											
Drugs, medicine											
Automobile insurance											
Auto maintenance fund											
Loans											
Alimony											
Child support/child care											
Other											
Other											
MONTHLY TOTALS											

confronted only when an old one dies. We suggest a third method: facing the certainty that appliances will break down in your fixed expenses. We call it an "appliance fund." How much should you put into the fund monthly? That depends on how new your equipment is, what you have, etc.

■ New roofs and other forms of home maintenance are inevitable, too. So are car repairs and maintenance. Budget for them monthly as fixed expenses.

■ You may have fixed expenses we haven't ever imagined. Use our categories as a guide. Delete those you don't need. Add your own.

■ Nobody's estimates are all correct. But you have to start somewhere. Usually, unless you have had a dramatic change of life-style (marriage/ divorce/ relocation, etc.) records from the past twelve months provide adequate working numbers. Plus common sense. If the roof is already leaking . . .

BEGINNING TO TRACK DAY-TO-DAY EXPENSES

If estimating fixed expenses is difficult, estimating day-to-day expenses may at first seem impossible. But you still have to do it. Make some estimates no matter how far off they may be. Over a period of time, you will become much better at it. What's more, we promise you an amazing thing invariably happens simply because you *are* estimating and keeping track of expenses: *You will spend less.*

You spend money in one of two ways for day-to-day expenses: by cash or by check. If you have written a check, you should be able to identify exactly what the money was spent on. You'll either have a bill (even if it is a credit card bill that itemizes seven different categories of expenses) or you'll know that $18.50 to the dry cleaner was for dry cleaning. If there's any question about what a check paid for, get in the habit of noting that in your checkbook.

Cash is harder to track. One of the reasons it seems to

go so fast is you can never remember what you spent it on. But to control and plan your spending budget, you must know. The solution is a notebook. If you are married, two of them—one his, one hers. Actually, since a number of tips in the chapters preceding this suggested you carry a notebook, you may not need a new one. One small notebook for all purposes is fine.

Will you feel silly writing down 50 cents when you buy your morning paper? Or $4.50 for lunch at McDonald's? If you do, remember how silly you have felt every time you ran out of money four days before next payday. Which is worse?

For at least three months, make a daily record of where every dollar goes. Go ahead and round off to dollars when the tab at the supermarket comes to $29.36. But if you spend 50 cents a day on a newspaper, 300 days a year, that's $150. You should know where $150 goes. Keep track of those expenses, down to the bar of candy you treat yourself to a couple of times a week.

Most people who keep a daily diary of cash expenditures for the first time are in for some big surprises. Back in the introduction, we cited the example of a Chicago friend who never thought much about the money he spent in "incidental" magazine purchases. When he started keeping a diary, he suddenly realized that magazines were costing him nearly $90.00 a month. He didn't give up the magazines, but he did decide to subscribe to the ones that were most important to him instead of buying them at his newsstand. That one small change saved him more than $400 a year.

Just by keeping a cash diary, nearly everyone becomes more conscious of spending patterns and more careful about purchases. Of course you'll forget to enter something from time to time. At the end of every day, examine what you have written down and think about what's missing. It will take a minute. Do it.

At the end of every day, week, or, if you prefer, every month, transfer all of the cash expenditures in your notebook to the appropriate individual Category Records we'll discuss shortly. At the same time, transfer all of the expenditures made by check to the same Category Rec-

Day-to-Day Expense Worksheet

	Jan.	Feb.	Mar.	Apr.	May	Jun.	July	Aug.	Sep.	Oct.	Nov.	Dec.	Yearly total
(A) Enter monthly income from Income Worksheet													
(B) Enter fixed expenses from Fixed Income Worksheet													
(C) Subtract B from A: Available for day-to-day expenses													
Day-to-day expenses:													
(1) Food/ groceries/ supermarket													

(2) Other house expenses												
(3) Clothing												
His												
Hers												
Children												
(4) Personal expenses and allowances												
His												
Hers												
Children												
(5) Transportation/gas/commuting												
(6) Furniture/equipment												
(7) Contributions/gifts												
(8) Vacation fund												
(9) Entertainment												

(continued)

(10) Subscriptions ———————————————————————

(11) Dry cleaning/laundry ———————————————————————

(12) Hobbies/lessons ———————————————————————

(13) Other ———————————————————————

(14) Other ———————————————————————

(D) Total day-to-day expenses ———————————————————————

(E) Subtract D from C—and don't panic! ═══════════════════

ords. Most people find it easiest to do this at least weekly. A month's worth of scribbled notes is hard to deal with at one time.

BUDGETING FOR DAY-TO-DAY EXPENSES

The checks you have written and your cash diaries are going to help you get a much better fix on day-to-day expenses. Ultimately, you may want to give up the cash diary and simply keep track of how much cash you spend in a month. By that point, you may be able to estimate cash expense categories accurately enough.

At this point, you can't. To prove that to yourself, start estimating expenses on the Day-to-Day Expense Worksheet on pages 208–210.

Examine the worksheet. You'll see at the top a quick way to figure out how much you have available for day-to-day expenses on a monthly basis. But for now, don't worry about that number. Instead, make an honest effort to estimate and budget in the suggested categories—and anything else you can think of. Don't set budget amounts that you know you won't be able to achieve. Be realistic. And one of your categories, at least in the beginning, should be "things I forgot or didn't know about."

Within the first month, you will add categories that you didn't remember at first. That's normal. Keep refining and changing the basic worksheet. You'll do that very often in the beginning, and far less often after a few months.

The categories we suggest are numbered to make it easier to refer to specific suggestions about a few of them.

(1) Food and groceries are probably your biggest cash expense, and definitely worth breaking down further. If you save the tapes from supermarkets, drugstores, and warehouse clubs, you can learn some fascinating things about your spending patterns at the end of every month. Especially if you use a giant supermarket, you might discover that 30 percent of what you thought of as food

expenses actually was spent on such things as cosmetics, soft drinks, and pet food.

Do you want to know that? Of course you do. Remember, no one else is looking. If $500 worth of soft drinks and ice cream a year is interfering with achieving long-term goals, you might want to cut back. You know your own habits; make up two or three subcategories and track your expenses in each.

(2) House expenses are a fuzzy area between a day-to-day and a fixed expense. We would describe a new roof as a fixed expense you should budget for in a "home maintenance fund" and a major home improvement such as a new bedroom as a fixed expense in the "saving for goals" category. Everything else, including cleaning supplies and help, goes here.

(3) Do you want to use subcategories to track clothing expenses individually? You decide. You could look at shoes for the kids and necessary clothing for work as fixed expenses, but you do have some control over them.

(4) Everyone deserves some personal money that doesn't have to be accounted for to anyone else. Work on this with your spouse and your children. Without their agreement, your family's budget won't work.

(5) Transportation should include tolls, parking, gas, bus fares, etc.—what's not in your auto maintenance fund.

(6) Furniture/equipment: Again, maybe one of your long-term goals was to completely redecorate or carpet your house. Otherwise, a variable expense because you could, if necessary, do without or buy secondhand.

(7) Contributions/gifts. Many people consider certain contributions as fixed expenses. Move them back to the previous worksheet. Otherwise, list here whatever isn't included under personal expenses and allowances.

(8–14) You'll probably want to break these expenses down differently. This is your plan, not ours. Don't try to use the sample worksheets we have printed here; the pages are too small in any case. Type or write out your own full-size worksheet. If you have access to a computer, by all means use it.

You should probably budget the same amount, month

by month, for most day-to-day expenses. Your expenses for food won't vary much, nor will allowances for kids. But this is your decision to make. If you have promised the kids two weeks at camp next summer, you had better save and budget for that expense on a monthly basis before they leave. If you would like to go to Hawaii in August but have already decided that will depend on how big a bonus you get in June, you can put the Hawaii expenses down when they will be incurred—if you go.

Okay, ready or not—using all the past records you can find, taking into account everything you know about what you and other family members will be doing in the next year, and *not* underestimating—put in your numbers and add them up.

THE MOMENT YOU'VE BEEN DREADING? RELAX

When you subtract D from C, do you get a row of minuses? Many, if not most, people do when they start a budget for the first time. But look on the bright side. Suppose you hadn't come this far in the process. Eventually, wouldn't you be a lot worse off not knowing that your spending needs exceeded your income?

Unfortunately, unlike the Federal government, you can't sell bonds and print more money when you spend more than you take in. You don't have any choice. You've got to go back and examine every fixed expense, every day-to-day expense, and every possible source of income. One way or another, you must have a balanced budget.

We made this the appendix in a book filled with tips on saving money because, by now, you may have some new ideas on how to cut various expenses. As you go back and examine each fixed expense, see if there aren't tips that can help—in the chapters on reducing insurance premiums, holding down utility and house expenses, etc. If your supermarket bills averaged $300 a month last year, can you save $30.00 to $50.00 of that by buying in bulk, joining a warehouse club, and using other tips in Chapter 1? Will that trip you're planning cost as much if you use a consolidator for airline tickets?

You may have to revise some of your long-term goals. It may not have been realistic to believe you could save $30,000 for a down payment on a new home in only three years. If you wait five years instead, you'll have to save only $6,000 a year ($500 a month) instead of $10,000 a year ($833 a month). If that $333 balances your budget and you can't make it up elsewhere, you don't have much choice. Be stubborn about long-term goals, though. There are so many better ways for most people to cut back on other expenses; first try every penny-pinching idea possible.

Too many people try it the reverse way. Maybe that raise will be larger than expected. Maybe business will improve and there will be more commission checks.

"Maybe" isn't good enough. Unless you have a definite, realistic plan you are positive will increase your income significantly, don't make the mistake of adjusting income upward so that your budget balances. It won't happen.

YOU'VE BALANCED YOUR BUDGET . . . NOW WHAT?

Congratulations. You actually have a budget plan. You know basically how you want to spend and save the money you have coming in. You understand that your plan won't work exactly the way you have it outlined right now. You realize you are in for a lot of changes, and that the first few months of living with a budget are the toughest.

What's next? Quite a bit of record keeping. A computer makes it easier, and there are a number of good, inexpensive budget software packages. You can buy one of them and skip the rest of this chapter, because just about all bookkeeping methods of family budgeting are essentially the same. What you have done up to this point was necessary whether you were going to use a computer or not, and probably just as easy to do with an old-fashioned pencil and a few pieces of paper.

If you don't have a computer, never mind. They save time, but there's nothing you can't accomplish just as well the old-fashioned way. Most stationery stores sell budget books—more or less blank pages with numbered lines and room for entries that describe an expenditure, the amount spent, and the month in which it was spent. Or see pages 218–222 for samples of the two forms we recommend (Category Record of Expenditures and Summary Record of Expense Categories), copy them using your own categories, and then make a lot of machine copies.

Remember you can start in any month—it doesn't have to be January. Whatever month you choose, do the following:

- Devote one page or sheet for each category of your fixed and day-to-day expenses. On this category record, you'll list all expenditures made within that category during the next twelve months. You'll have records of each of these expenditures in either your cash notebook, credit card and department store bills, or your checkbook. If you find an expenditure that doesn't fit in one of your categories, make up a new category or broaden the definition of an existing one. *Every* expenditure you make should ultimately find its way onto a category record.

  Use common sense and don't keep records just to keep records. Tote up the total your notebook says you spent on lunches for a month and enter that one amount in whatever category record in which you've decided to put lunches. You want to make sure that the amount of every expenditure you make ultimately is accounted for someplace, but you don't care that one day you had tuna fish and the next day ham on rye. Consolidating many individual expenditures (but always within a month's time) is fine.

  Some individual category records will run to several pages during the year, others may consist of just a few entries. The form is always the same though; see the example on pages 218 and 219.

- At the end of each month, after you have filled out and

totaled each category record, transfer those totals to a
Summary Record. The summary record (see example
on pages 220, 221 and 222) should list each of your
expense categories in the left-hand column.

- Each month (or in the middle of the month if you know
  you are in trouble), compare actual expenditures against
  the Fixed Expense and Day-to-Day Expense Worksheets you started out with. During the first couple of
  months, keep revising those worksheets as you get a
  more realistic idea of what expenditures are necessary
  within categories, but make certain that as you revise
  them you still keep your overall budget in balance.

- A number of your fixed and even your day-to-day
  monthly expenses are actually "accruals"—amounts you
  are setting aside for such things as paying a big annual
  bill, covering yourself in case you need a new appliance,
  or meeting long-term goals. This money should be
  deposited each month in a bank savings or money
  market account, separate from your checking account.
  You'll have to establish some way to keep track of
  accruals; one way to do it is suggested below.

- Keep a separate record, month by month, of income.
  The format of this record is exactly the same as the
  Summary Record. Compare this monthly against your
  Income Worksheet.

Within a couple of months, you should have established
spending patterns and begun to adjust some of them so
that you have more to spend in other areas. At this point,
you should be able to stop revising the numbers within
different categories and start using the monthly expenditure numbers in your often-revised Expense Worksheets
as serious budget goals.

That, after all, is what an operating budget is—a way to
control expenses by setting target expenditures and then
sticking to them.

HOW TO HANDLE ACCRUALS

The easiest way to *explain* how to handle all the different expense categories in which you make monthly deposits for savings and/or future expenditures is to tell you to open a separate savings account for each one—one for "Saving for Goals"; one for "Life Insurance Premium"; one for "Appliance Fund"; etc. You put money in each account as budgeted each month. When the expense or the goal comes due, you take the money out.

Since you don't want to have twenty-two separate savings accounts, that is impossible. What you can do, however, is make a list of all the accrual categories included in one savings or money market fund. Make monthly deposits for each one as budgeted in your Expense Worksheets. As money is taken out, check to see how close to your annual budget number the actual expenditure is. With any luck, the refrigerator won't break down the same time the water heater has to be replaced. If it does, you may not have any choice but to temporarily rob Peter (the vacation fund) to pay Paul (the appliance fund).

At the end of every month, take a look at Fixed Expense Worksheet A (the one that lists expenditures in the month they are actually due) to make sure your savings account can handle what's coming up. Within time, this account should provide far greater protection than that. When it includes enough to take care of upcoming fixed expenses accrued for, as well as a three-month emergency fund (enough money for you and your family to live on for three months without salary checks), it is time to transfer money out of the savings account into other types of investments.

At the end of every year, or more often if you like, prepare a summary record like the one on pages 220–222, using the exact amounts actually spent (not budgeted) in each of the accrual accounts. When you do this at the end of the year, it will be a final, accurate record of all of your actual expenditures by category. It will help you revise budget categories for the next year.

You may have a lucky year in which not a penny is spent

Category Record of Expenditures: Clothing

Expenditure/date	Jan.	Feb.	Mar.	Apr.	May	Jun.	July	Aug.	Sep.	Oct.	Nov.	Dec.
Scarf, hers 1/3	$18											
Blouse, hers 1/3	22											
Hosiery, hers 1/1	30											
2 dress shirts, 1/3 his	54											
Sneakers, hers 1/6		32										
Blazer, his 3/12			190									
(and so on. At bottom												
of each page, total for each month												
and transfer to Summary Record)												